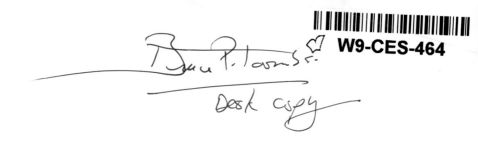

A Guided Tour of Selections from Aristotle's *Nicomachean Ethics*

Christopher Biffle
San Bernardino Valley College

Mayfield Publishing Company
Mountain View, California
London • Toronto

Copyright © 1991 by Mayfield Publishing Company

Library of Congress Cataloging-in-Publication Data

Aristotle.
   [Nicomachean ethics. English. Selections]
   A guided tour of selections from Aristotle's Nicomachean ethics /
[edited by] Christopher Biffle.
      p.   cm.
   Translation of selections from: Nicomachean ethics.
   Includes bibliographical references.
   ISBN 0-87484-895-4
   1. Ethics.   I. Biffle, Christopher. II. Title.
B430.A5B5413   1990
171'/3--dc20   90-45138
                                                  CIP

Manufactured in the United States of America
10 9 8 7 6

Mayfield Publishing Company
1280 Villa Street
Mountain View, California 94041

Sponsoring editor, James Bull; managing editor, Linda Toy; production
editor, Carol Zafiropoulos; manuscript editor, Loralee Windsor; text
designer, Jeanne M. Schreiber; production artist, Jean Mailander; cover
designer, Kacey Fitzpatrick; cover image, The Bettmann Archive. The
text was set in 10/12 Palatino and printed on 50# Finch Opaque by
Malloy Lithographing.

CONTENTS

PREFACE

One of the hardest tasks in preparing this tour of the *Nicomachean Ethics* was deciding what to leave out. Publishing costs being what they are, I had to design a short tour of a long work. I believe I have selected material that would be central to most classroom presentations. This includes major portions of Books I through IV and Book X, along with Aristotle's discussion of theoretical and practical wisdom in Book VI, moral strength and weakness in Book VII, and aspects of friendship in Books VIII and IX. I also wanted to give some sense of the *Ethics* as a whole. The best solution seemed to be to include summaries of each book as part of the Introduction.

My goals in this book are the same as in the others in the Guided Tour series. I want students to bring books to class that are as marked up as their teachers'. I want to give students good things to think about as they read and useful things to write about after they have read. I want to provide a template for the kind of reflection, annotating, and slow, close reading that is necessary to understand philosophical classics.

The annotation and fill-in-the-blank exercises involve underlining or paraphrasing passages from Aristotle, evaluating the strengths and weaknesses of his arguments, creating original examples to illustrate these arguments, and trying to solve the problems Aristotle tries to solve. This last exercise is the unifying intellectual task of this tour. At the end of many chapters, I frame the question or problem that Aristotle answers in the next chapter and invite students to match wits with, as Aquinas put it, The Philosopher. This seems to me to focus student reading and generate appreciation for the elegance of Aristotle's solutions. Some chapters have no pedagogical aids so that the student can practice annotation skills learned in other parts of the tour. The exercise in Appendix A, "Writing a Short Essay about Aristotle," is a fairly complete example of the kind of work one needs to do before starting to write many kinds of papers in philosophy.

Each instructor will know how best to use this book, but I encourage its use for class work as well as homework. Class discussion seems to me to be livelier if it is preceded by students working in pairs or in small groups on selected reading or writing tasks.

The techniques I've designed have had their critics, though not nearly as many as I had imagined. The main criticism seems to be that I have simplified and diluted the classics. Unsurprisingly, I don't agree. Students who complete this tour will not have been able to skim read, will have worked through any number of problems fairly carefully, will have had to reread slowly many times, will, in short, have given the classics the kind of attention they deserve.

Acknowledgments

I must thank Jack Jackson, Will Brunson, and Gary Love. Jack did hard work in a short time on the introduction, Will helped me formulate responses to reviewers of the original manuscript, and Gary organized the bibliography and worked tirelessly with me on the translation. Plato says the beautiful is the difficult; my three partners were beautiful and never difficult.

I would also like to thank my colleagues who served as reviewers: William C. Brunson, Crafton Hills College; Angelo Bucchino, Frostburg State University; William Kinnaman, Community College of Rhode Island; William Lawhead, University of Mississippi; Donald Palmer, College of Marin; Charles M. Young, The Claremont Graduate School.

About the Translation

The text is based on F.H. Peter's nineteenth-century translation. I have modernized his punctuation and substituted words and phrases more appropriate for the modern reader. Clarifying comments enclosed in these brackets { } are my own.

This book is dedicated to one of my oldest friends, William Colton Dickinson. At our first encounter twenty-five years ago, Bill changed my life. Before meeting him, I loved to argue. During a few late night sessions in Santa Cruz, Bill quickly taught me that if philosophy meant winning arguments, I had no future in the game. He has been teaching me good things ever since.

To the Student
An Introduction to Aristotle

Before you begin this guided tour of the *Nicomachean Ethics*, there are several things you should know. First I will tell you about Aristotle's life, and then I will explain several key concepts in his philosophy as they apply to his *Ethics*. Next I will describe the curious format of the *Nicomachean Ethics* and summarize each of its ten books. Finally I will give you some advice about reading Aristotle. Because I want you to think as you read, at several points in this introduction there will be an opportunity to respond to what I have said.

Aristotle's Life

Aristotle was born in 384 B.C. in Stagira, a northern Greek colony bordering on Macedonia. His father, Nicomachus, was a physician in the court of the king of Macedonia. These two simple facts, his birthplace and his father's occupation, help us understand several important aspects of Aristotle's life:

1. Although he died early in Aristotle's life, his father's profession probably had some influence on Aristotle's interest in biology and the world known by the senses.
2. His connection with Macedonia led him always to be an outsider when considering Athens and the life of that city.
3. Aristotle's later tutoring of Alexander the Great is rooted in the simple fact that Aristotle's father was the doctor of Alexander's great grandfather.

When Aristotle was about seventeen years old, in 367 B.C., he traveled south to Athens to study at Plato's famous Academy. Since he remained at the Academy for twenty years, it is safe to assume that this early period in Aristotle's life was formed to a large degree by his relationship with Plato and Platonic thought.

After Plato's death in 347 B.C., Aristotle left Athens and the Academy. Scholars offer several possible reasons for this departure. Perhaps Aristotle did not approve of the approach of Plato's successors. Perhaps there were ill feelings and resentment toward the outsider from Macedonia. Perhaps Aristotle was opening up an "extension branch" of Plato's Academy. Whatever the reason, Aristotle traveled and taught in the eastern Aegean, eventually founding a new school at Mytilene on the island of Lesbos.

A few years later, in 343 or 342 B.C., King Philip of Macedonia asked Aristotle to tutor his young son, Alexander. Now Aristotle had an opportunity to try to achieve Plato's ideal of educating a "philosopher king" by taking this twelve- or thirteen-year-old lad under his tutelage. However, there is conflicting evidence concerning the relationship between Aristotle and his young pupil. Some say Alexander's education did not shape his life as it could have. Alexander's vision of an empire is certainly different from Aristotle's vision of society, which seems never to have expanded beyond the city-state. Yet there are stories of an older Alexander ordering his troops to send back to his former mentor biological specimens found during the conquest of new lands. After a few years with this special pupil, Aristotle moved back to Stagira, his original home.

At the height of the Alexandrian Empire, outsiders, specifically Macedonians, were safe in Athens. Aristotle returned there in 335–334 B.C. to found his school, the Lyceum. This school seemed to emphasize descriptive analysis over the dialectic of question and answer that was Plato's lasting contribution to philosophy. Aristotle spent the mornings walking with students and discussing philosophy. Because of this practice, philosophy at the Lyceum was called *peripatetic*, the Greek word for "walking around."

When Alexander died in 323 B.C. there was a resurgence of anti-Macedonian sentiment in Athens. Aristotle was charged with impiety. Plato's teacher, Socrates, had been accused of impiety and sentenced to death for the charge. Aristotle decided not to give Athens, as he said, "the opportunity to sin twice against philosophy" and fled to the city of Chalcis. Aristotle died the next year still observing the world around him. He was at work in his final days on a study of the tides in the gulf of Euripus.

The Range of Aristotle's Contributions

The era in which Aristotle lived has been called the first "axial age." That is, at that time human culture seemed to make a gigantic intellectual leap in various places around the globe—especially India, Greece, and China. Aristotle lived in one of those hot spots of radical cultural and intellectual change. Surely the constellation of Socrates, his pupil, Plato, and Plato's pupil, Aristotle, constitutes a crucial pivot or axis in Western thought. After Aristotle, most of the dominant philosophical trends in every age in the West contain either a response to or a continuation of his concerns.

Aristotle's interests in philosophy ranged even wider than Plato's. Aristotle had a passion for the concrete, the physical, all that can be known by the senses. One critic argues that the central distinction between Aristotle and Plato is that the latter took mathematics as his ideal and the former took biology.[1] Plato thus prefers truths about the aspects of reality that are unchanging, perfect, and lifeless; Aristotle prefers truths about the aspects of reality that are imperfect, changing, and living. One of Aristotle's great achievements was to begin to categorize and describe the physical universe. He made such important contributions to biology, meteorology, geology, and botany that he is called the Father of Science. Aristotle can also be called one of the inventors of logic. To a large degree he advanced and systematized the rules for rational thinking. Rhetoric, poetics, and theory of knowledge were other areas of interest to Aristotle. His ethical reflections and analysis of daily life make his investigation of human behavior classic. Aristotle's philosophical concerns have been transmitted through Arab scholars and Thomas Aquinas, among others, to form a dominant philosophical foundation of modern thought.

The Beginning of a Dialogue

Before we go further, think for a few moments and write down some of the things you just learned about Aristotle. _____

_____

_____

_____.

Now that you have had a brief description of Aristotle's life and the range of his contributions, here are a few signposts to guide you through his thought.

Politics and Society

Aristotle's *Nicomachean Ethics* begins and ends with references to political science. To Aristotle, human beings are political and social beings. Moral action is possible only within society and community.

Isolated individual activity is not the realm of ethics or, for that matter, of human existence. Many modern existentialists take isolation, alienation, "forlornness" as central characteristics of the human situation. These concepts are alien to Aristotle. At the end of Jean Paul Sartre's *No Exit* a character announces, "Hell is other people." Toward the end of the *Nichomachean Ethics* Aristotle considers the question of how many friends we should have. He considers many alternatives, but he never wonders if we should have no friends. For Aristotle, to be human is to be with others.

Plato and Aristotle on the Good

In the "Allegory of the Cave" Plato compares the Form of the Good to the sun; just as the sun makes sight possible, the Form of the Good makes knowledge possible. All particular good things, the good in a work of art, the good in a just law, the good in a noble human action, are shadows or copies of the Form of the Good. The Form of the Good is goodness itself, perfect, eternal, nonphysical, unchanging goodness. If all good things in our world vanished, the Form of the Good and the other Forms (the Form of Courage, the Form of Justice, the Form of Human Nature) would remain in a higher world. The realm of Forms is the invisible, eternal, higher world of which this world is a poor copy, and the Form of the Good is the highest of all Forms.

Because I want you to think about Aristotle's concept of the good for yourself later on the tour, I will say only this about his view: For Aristotle the good, which we will here call the chief good, is part of the human realm and is implied in all human actions. While there is a genuine question in Plato about how much we can know about the Form of the Good, Aristotle gives a simple, general definition of the chief good, which he says all men acknowledge. For Plato, if we are ever to truly know the Form of the Good, our purified souls must separate from our bodies after death. For Aristotle, a person of good character realizes the chief good in every virtuous action. (Note again that I have not defined what this chief good is for Aristotle. That will be your task after you have read the opening pages of his *Ethics*.)

Two Kinds of Ethical Systems

Ethics is the study of right and wrong human actions. In ethics we distinguish between deontological and teleological statements. The word *deontological* comes from the Greek word *deontos,* meaning duty. A deontological approach to ethics therefore emphasizes the connection between right action and duty. An individual obeys the Ten Commandments, from one deontological perspective, because it is simply right to do so. It is our duty as human beings. The word teleological comes from the Greek *telos,* meaning end or purpose. A teleological approach to ethics therefore emphasizes the connection between right action and the result or end of right action.[2] From one teleological perspective, an individual obeys the Ten Commandments because if the individual does obey, he or she goes to Heaven.

Aristotle begins the *Ethics* with assertions that link "the good" and the "aim or the goal" of things and actions. "Every art and every kind of scientific inquiry and also every action and choice, seem to aim at some good. Thus it has been well said that the good is that at which everything aims." Our actions have ends or goals, and later in the *Ethics* Aristotle identifies the end or *telos* of the moral life as happiness. For Aristotle happiness is an end in itself because it is never chosen as a means to something else. For example, contrast our pursuit of happiness with our pursuit of money. We seek money not for itself but as a means of purchasing food, shelter, and goods. We seek happiness for itself alone; once we have happiness we do not use it to achieve anything further or better.

The Soul

Another important concept to discuss before you begin your journey through the *Nicomachean Ethics* is the idea of the soul. Plato argued that the soul has three parts: appetite (physical desire and longing); the spirited element (the place of several kinds of strong emotions); and reason. These three parts are in conflict in humans, and the goal of philosophy is to have reason rule and restore harmony. Aristotle divides the soul into only two parts: the irrational and the rational. The irrational part of the soul is "vegetative" or "nutritive," that is, it nourishes. This part is common to all life. There is another part of the irrational soul, however, that does have a rational component that can be persuaded by reason. This is the appetitive part (Book I). Aristotle also divides the rational part of the soul into two components: one that contemplates things that cannot be other than what they are and one that contemplates things that can be other than what they are (Book VI). This is Aristotle's rather complex way of saying that we can reason about the universe (which cannot be other than what it is) or about our daily life (which can be other than what it is). These two parts of the rational soul are the "scientific" and the "calculative," respectively. In essence, a large part of Aristotle's *Ethics* is a description of the best and worst uses of the rational and irrational parts of the soul.

Doctrine of the Mean

Another crucial idea in the *Nicomachean Ethics* is the doctrine of the mean. For every virtue there are two vices, one of excess and the other of deficiency. In other words, for every action or feeling we can do what is too much, too little, or just right. (Goldilocks was a natural Aristotelian.) We can be foolhardy, cowardly, or courageous; we can be self-indulgent, insensible, or self-controlled; we can be short-tempered, apathetic, or patient. Aristotle wisely points out that what is extreme for one person may not be extreme for another. He further points out that we cannot expect the precision from ethics that we can from science or mathematics. Updating an example Aristotle uses, if ten pounds of food is too much for an athlete to eat every day and two pounds is too little, it does not follow that six pounds (the mathematical mean) is exactly right. Six pounds may be too little for a weightlifter but too much for a marathon runner. According to Aristotle, it is the mean relative to each individual that the individual should seek. Thus the mean is something like a metaphor, not to be taken absolutely or literally but still valuable as a general target at which to aim all our actions.

When we observe the mean we are acting virtuously. To be virtuous in Aristotle's sense is to use our human gifts correctly. Thus virtue is often translated as excellence. In the Aristotelian sense the virtue of a racehorse is its ability to run fast; its speed is its unique excellence. The virtue of a knife is its ability to cut; its sharpness is its unique excellence. Thus to Aristotle virtue is a remarkably wide-ranging concept that could include everything from excellent horses to excellent knives. Aristotle's word for virtue (*arete*) has a much broader scope than the word virtue is sometimes taken to have in the twentieth century. For many modern people, virtue is closely associated with sexual morality. To Aristotle people are virtuous if they have been guided by reason to choose the mean and thus realize their full range of potentialities; a modern view might hold a person virtuous if he or she is chaste.

The Form of the Nicomachean Ethics

It is important to realize before your reading of the *Nicomachean Ethics* that this text was not intended for publication in any modern sense of that term. Most critics agree that what we have is something like a set of lecture notes collected and edited at a later time (perhaps by his son, Nicomachus to whom the work is dedicated). This is important because it explains several obvious characteristics of the *Ethics*. The analysis is often abrupt, occasionally circular, sometimes dense, and at other times simply poorly organized. In fact the notes appear to have been accumulated over a period of years and occasionally contain two or more approaches to the same topic. This tour was designed, if not to solve all the difficulties ahead, at least to help you think through them.

Look back at your underlinings and margin notes and try to summarize one key idea from each of the last six sections.

The sections are "Politics and Society," "Plato and Aristotle on the Good," "Two Kinds of Ethical Systems," "The Soul," "Doctrine of the Mean," and "The Form of the Nicomachean Ethics." In the same order, an important idea in the first section was _____

_____.

An important concept in the second section was _____

_____.

What I noted in the third section was _____

_____.

What you seemed to be saying in the fourth section was _____

_____.

The essential idea in the fifth section was _____

_____.

The key idea in the sixth section was _____

_____.

Summaries of the Books

Book I: The Goal of Life

Aristotle begins by claiming that the good is the end or aim of life. This concept applies to all human conduct in society, and, therefore, the science of politics is the study of the chief good for humans. Politics is not an exact science, however, and should be studied only after considerable experience in life. What is the end or goal of human life? Happiness.[3] But what is happiness? In responding to this question, Aristotle begins to distance himself from his teacher, Plato, and Plato's theory of Forms. Aristotle says that the good for humans is the activity of the human soul in accordance with virtue. After distinguishing the two parts of the soul, Aristotle describes virtue as either intellectual or moral. Intellectual virtue deals with excellence of the powers of reasoning (like prudence and theoretical wisdom). Moral virtues deal with the control of desires and emotions by a rational standard.

Book II: Moral Virtues

Aristotle continues by saying that moral goodness is the result of habit and practice. We become virtuous by doing virtuous actions. Further, moral qualities are destroyed by excess and deficiency.

Although pleasure and pain can be indicators of moral progress in life, virtue is not a feeling or a faculty but a disposition. Virtue avoids the extremes of excess and deficiency and seeks the middle, the mean. Aristotle provides a descriptive list of virtues that are means between two extremes.

Book III: Moral Responsibility

Book III begins by distinguishing voluntary and involuntary acts. Moral goodness is limited to voluntary acts of individuals who know the particular circumstances of an action. Thus moral conduct implies choice. Desires are not the result of choice. Choice involves deliberation, and deliberation concerns the means toward an end, not the end itself. Thus the moral life involves "taking care" with deliberation. Aristotle ends the book with descriptions of two virtues: courage and self-control. Courage is a mean between cowardliness and foolhardiness in response to things that cause fear. Self-control is a mean between self-indulgence and insensibility in regard to physical pleasure.

Book IV: Other Moral Virtues

Book IV defines generosity as the mean between extravagance and greed in attitudes toward money. Magnificence is a mean between gaudiness and pettiness in more financially significant endeavors. Patience is a mean between bad temper and apathy. Some virtues have no name, but the excesses are easily identified. For example, there is, as everyone knows, a mean between boasting and understatement. Aristotle continues the list of moral virtues and concludes with the assertion that modesty is not a virtue and is only appropriate in youth.

Book V: Justice

Justice and injustice are ambiguous notions. Nevertheless, Aristotle presses through the ambiguity to describe injustice as unfair action. Conversely, justice is fairness and the ability to remain within the boundaries of the law. As a voluntary obedience to the law, justice includes all the moral virtues. Justice also deals with the proportional distribution of goods and services. This emphasis on proportion leads Aristotle to articulate the standard of value for services that are unequally distributed. That standard is "demand." And "demand" is represented by money.

After discussing political and domestic justice, Aristotle asks "can one be unjust to oneself?" The response lets Aristotle again affirm his social starting point. Justice and injustice must always involve more than one person. That is why punishment is undertaken by the state. In a metaphorical sense Aristotle is willing to let injustice be an individual affair. Yet even in the metaphor there is community; injustice is then done to parts of the self at the expense of other parts of the self. The self, then, is modeled on a community of interrelated units. This book completes Aristotle's reflections on moral virtues.

Book VI: Intellectual Virtues

Moral virtues have been described as a mean between two extremes: excess and deficiency. In Book VI Aristotle describes the rational principle by which the mean is selected. Since there are contemplative and calculative parts of the soul, there are different modes for this rational activity. There are five ways that the mind arrives at intellectual virtue: scientific knowledge, technical skill (art), prudence (translated in many places on the tour as *practical wisdom*), intuition, and theoretical wisdom. Prudence (practical wisdom) is manifested in the political sciences. Since Aristotle asserted that politics is the arena of investigation for ethics, prudence takes on a significant role in Aristotle's list of intellectual virtues.

Book VII: Self-Control and Self-Indulgence

Three states of character that are to be avoided are: vice, loss of self-control, and what Aristotle calls "brutishness." Self-control is lost when one is pulled into an action one knows to be wrong. In Book VII Aristotle describes pleasure and various popular views concerning it. To Aristotle pleasure may be either appropriate or harmful. Reflection on pleasure and pain is the task of the political philosopher. Once again Aristotle affirms the necessary social and political arena for the application of ethics.

Book VIII: Friendship

Aristotle's next step in the analysis of virtue is to deal with friendship. Friendship is both necessary and natural for human life. There are three kinds of friendship, based on utility, pleasure, and the desire for the good of the other. Friendships based strictly on usefulness or pleasure, as well as the friendships of bad persons, will not endure as do the true friendships between people who are good. Friendship implies some sort of equality or desire for equality. When there is great inequality in a relationship, friendship is impossible. Friendship is based on and assumes the existence of community. Thus friendship is the virtue that allows Aristotle's concern for society and the body politic to remain at center stage in his ethic.

Book IX: Analysis of Friendship Continued

In Book IX Aristotle continues his discussion of friendship, addressing practical problems and apparent paradoxes. Competing claims by several friends, the priorities of friendship, as well as the extent and length of friendship—especially when one of the persons has changed dramatically—are some of the concrete problems he addresses. Furthermore, says Aristotle, feelings toward friends reflect feelings about oneself. This leads him to ask about self-love. He discusses in what sense self-love is and is not justifiable. He then considers whether friends are necessary for happiness and how many friends one should have.

Book X: Pleasure and Happiness

Pleasure is important for ethics because it has a powerful influence on virtues and the happy life. In Book X Aristotle describes the conflicting views of the values of pleasure. Pleasure is not a process. It is complete in itself at any given moment. Pleasure perfects activities and therefore perfects life, since life is activity. Since activities differ, so do pleasures. Intellectual pleasures are superior to sensual ones. Happiness is the leisurely activity of the true self and this true self is reason. Perfect happiness consists in the life of thought contemplating the truth. However, because humans have composite natures, people derive other kinds of happiness in external things and in the practice of the moral virtues. Education and training in virtue should be provided for all people by the laws of the state. Once again Aristotle asserts that students of ethics must apply themselves to politics.

Advice about Reading Aristotle

A new friend told me recently that he had a graduate class in Greek during which the first five weeks were spent on the first line of Homer's *Iliad*. The history and meaning of each word were fully explored. At the end of the fifth week, the teacher solemnly announced, "Ladies and gentlemen, reading Greek is the art of reading slowly." Something similar might be said of philosophy. The worst readers are the fastest; the best readers are laboriously slow. This tour is designed to undo all the good work of your grammar school teachers who praised you for reading many pages quickly. In this book you will learn how to read at a snail's pace, and perhaps you will slowly become wise.

Here are the opening sentences of the *Nicomachean Ethics*. Underline and then ponder the key words. If you find yourself staring off into space, you are on the right track. Try to think of examples of what Aristotle means.

> Every art and every kind of scientific inquiry and also every action and choice, seem to aim at some good. Thus, it has been well said that the good is that at which everything aims.

Think about this and then say what you think Aristotle means. Then think of examples of an art[4] and an action and the good each aims at.

Aristotle seems to be saying _____

_____

_____.

An example of an art is _____ and the good at which

it aims is _____. An example of an action is

_____ and the good at which it aims is

_____.

A synonym for *good* as Aristotle uses the term is *goal*. Thus the goal of the art of religious sculpture might be to produce an image of a god. The good or goal of a craft like shoemaking would be to produce shoes. What good or goal does an exercise like jogging aim at?

The good of jogging might be _____ , or, looked at

in another way, it might be _____.

Now you are ready to complete this little chart. Add your own examples and the good each aims at. Don't worry if this takes you awhile. Think of it as "slow" practice.

Activities	Example	The Good	Example	The Good
Art	love poetry	wooing the beloved		
Craft	pottery	making pots		
Scientific Inquiry	meteorology	predicting the weather		
Action	writing this book	fan letters		
Choice	voting	a better government		

Now we are ready to go on to the second paragraph of the *Nicomachean Ethics.* Underline, write your own notes in the column, think of examples.

But there is a difference among these aims or ends. What is aimed at is sometimes an activity and sometimes a result or product of an activity. In this latter case where the aim or end is some product of an activity, the product is naturally superior to the activity itself.

What do you think this means?

I think he means _____
_____.

The phrase I understood the most clearly was, "_____
_____." This
means that _____.

An example would be _____
_____.

According to Aristotle, some activities, such as the pursuit of pure scientific knowledge, are ends in themselves. In other words, an astronomer studies the stars not for any other end than to know more about the stars. In fact Aristotle might argue that if an astronomer studied the stars for some other reason, like achieving fame or getting away from her husband or making a living, then she wouldn't really be an astronomer. She would be a fame seeker, an unhappy spouse, or a college employee.

Now look again at the third sentence, "In this latter case where the aim or end is some product of an activity, the product is naturally superior to the activity itself." Think of an activity that creates a product and explain in what sense the product might be said to be superior to the activity.

The activity I am thinking of is _____. The
product it produces is _____. The reason the
product might be said to be superior to the activity is _____
_____.

Think of the activity of chopping wood. The products that are created are logs for the fireplace. Unless we are at a dude ranch, chopping wood is not an end in itself. The logs are "superior" to the chopping because the hard work of chopping serves no purpose in itself; we chop wood to produce the logs that keep us warm on winter nights. What we really want are logs, not sweat. Once again think of an example of an activity and the product it produces and then try to apply my explanation to your example.

Take the activity _____. Its product
is _____. The product is superior to the activity

because _____.
The way the example of chopping and the logs produced applies to

this is _____.

Now you know some slow reading skills. Stop reading frequently and simply think about what Aristotle is saying, find your own examples, underline, write notes in the margin, and reread. It is better to read one sentence five times and understand it than to read five sentences once and be lost. Slow reading saves time.

Each book of the *Nicomachean Ethics* is divided into chapters. I have given each of these chapters a title in the form of a question. The question is often (but not always) answered in the opening paragraph. Use the title to guide your underlinings. For example, the title of the first chapter is "What do all human actions aim at?" You will be underlining Aristotle's answer to this question and a few of the key statements he uses to expand his answer. Don't underline everything! Use underlining to create an outline of the most important sentences and phrases. This will simplify rereading.

One of your major tasks ahead (beginning in the third chapter of Book I) will be to try to solve the same philosophical problems Aristotle tries to solve. As Aristotle says, "we become builders by building and harpers by harping." One becomes philosophical by trying to be philosophical.

Book I
The Goal of Life

1. What do all human actions aim at?

Every art and every kind of scientific inquiry and also every action and choice, seem to aim at some good. Thus it has been well said that the good is that at which everything aims.

There is a difference, however, among these aims or ends. What is aimed at is sometimes an activity and sometimes a result or product of an activity. In this latter case where the aim or end is some product of an activity, the product is naturally superior to the activity itself.

Since there are many kinds of actions and many arts and sciences, it follows that there are also many ends. Health is the end of medicine, ships are the end of shipbuilding, victory is the end of the art of war, and wealth is the end of economy.

When several of these activities are subordinated to a particular art—as the making of bridles and other trappings is subordinated to the art of horsemanship, and this in turn, along with all else that the soldier does, is subordinated to the art of war, and so on—the end of the master art is always more desired than the ends of the subordinate arts. The reason for this is that the subordinate arts are pursued for the sake of the master art. This is equally true whether the end is the activity or, as in cases just mentioned, in something beyond the activity.

Another example would be _____
_____
_____
is the end of _____
_____.

Pause here for a moment. Health, ships, victory, and wealth are all examples of what (one word)?

They are examples of _____s.

Look back at your underlinings and write down Aristotle's example of a master art and why it is preferred to his examples of subordinate arts. The master art is _____ and it is preferred to subordinate arts like _____ because _____.

In the next short section underline the key statements Aristotle makes in answer to the question posed in the chapter title.

2.   What science studies the chief good?

If in what we do there is some end that we wish for its own sake, choosing all other ends as a means to this one most desirable end, but each end is not desired as an end to something else and so on forever, because then our desire would be futile and pointless, this most desirable end will be the good or {better} the chief good.

The chief good is what we desire for
_____
_____
_____.

Surely from a practical point of view it is important for us to know this chief good because then, like archers shooting at a definite target, we shall be more likely to attain what we want. If this is true, we must try to indicate roughly what the chief good is, and first of all to which of the arts or sciences it belongs. It seems to belong to the art or science that most of all deserves the name of master art or master science.

Politics seems to answer to this description. Politics prescribes which of the sciences a state needs, and which each man shall study, and up to what point; and to politics we see subordinated even the highest arts, such as economy, oratory, and the art of war.

Since politics makes use of the other practical sciences, and since it further ordains what men are to do and from what to refrain, its end must include the ends of the others, and must be the proper good of man.

1094b

For though this good is the same for the individual and the state, yet the good of the state seems a more perfect thing both to attain and to safeguard; though it is good to attain the end for one man, it is far better to attain it for a people and nobler and more divine still to attain it for a nation.

This then is the aim of the present inquiry, which is a type of political inquiry.

Why is politics the science of the chief good, or, to put it another way, the end of all ends?

My answer is that _____

_____

_____.

Aristotle often divides a large topic into a number of sub-topics or a whole into its parts. What is an example of a whole and its parts in this section?

The first whole is _____ and the parts he

mentions are _____.

Aristotle says, " For though this good {the good of man} is the same for the individual and the state, yet the good of the state seems a more perfect thing both to attain and to safeguard; though it is good to attain the end for one man, it is far better to attain it for a people and nobler and more divine still to attain it for a nation."

This should not be too difficult for you to put in your own words.

He is saying _____

_____

_____.

What is your reaction to Aristotle thus far?

I think _____

_____

_____.

To get more out of my reading I could _____

_____.

Try your advice in the next section.

3.   Why can't the investigation of politics be exact?

We must be content if we can attain as much precision in our statement as the subject before us allows, because the same degree of precision is no more to be expected in all kinds of reasoning than in all kinds of manufactured articles.

Now what is noble and just, which is what politics deals with, is so various and so uncertain that some people think morality exists merely by custom and not as part of the nature of things.

There is also a similar uncertainty about what is good, because good things often do people harm: Men have before now been ruined by wealth and have lost their lives through courage.

The words "this kind" refer back to

_____

_____.

Because our subject and our data are of this kind, we must be content if we can indicate the truth roughly and in outline. Dealing with matters that are not amenable to unchanging laws and reasoning from premises that are only probable, we can only arrive at broad, general conclusions.

The reader, on his part, should take each of my statements in the same spirit because it is the mark of an educated man to require in each kind of inquiry only as much exactness as the subject allows: It is equally absurd to accept probable reasoning from a mathematician as to demand rigid scientific proof from an orator.

The two kinds of absurdity are _____ _____ and _____ _____.

Each man can form a judgment about what he knows, and he is called a good judge of a particular field when he has received education in that particular field. He is called a good judge in general when he has received a broad and well-rounded education. Thus a young man is not qualified to be a student of politics because he lacks broad experience of the affairs of life, which form the data and the subject matter of politics. Further, since a young man is apt to be swayed by his feelings, he will derive no benefit from a study whose aim is not knowledge but action.

1095a

In this respect immaturity in character is the same as immaturity in years because the young man's disqualification is a matter not of time but of the fact that feeling rules his life and directs all his desires. Men of this character turn the knowledge they get to no use in practice, as we see with those we call morally unstable; but those who direct their desires and actions by reason will gain much profit from the knowledge of these matters.

So much, then, by way of preface to the student, the spirit in which he must accept what we say, and the object that we propose to ourselves.

In the opening paragraphs of this chapter Aristotle gives reasons why this investigation cannot be exact.

The first reason is _____ _____.

The second is _____ _____.

I hope you underlined the three main topics that serve as a summary in the last paragraph. What do they signify?

The student of politics needs to be _____ . The spirit he should approach the subject with should be _____ .

And the object is, of course, _____ _____ .

Here is your first opportunity to practice solving the same problem as Aristotle. He has said that the good is what all human actions aim at. And the science of politics is the means to an end that is the highest and most inclusive good of all, the chief good. The obvious question is what would be the chief good?

"It does not seem simple to further define the chief good, the highest of all goods. Thinking about this carefully I would say the end that all human actions seem to aim at eventually would be

_____."

Aristotle's answer is surprisingly simple. Underline it in the next chapter.

4. What is the chief good, and what are some of the views about it?

Since all knowledge and all purpose aim at some good, what is this that we say is the aim of politics; or, in other words, what is the highest of all realizable goods?

As to its name, I suppose nearly all men are agreed, because the masses and men of culture alike declare that it is happiness and hold that to "live well" or to "do well" is the same as to be "happy."

But they differ as to what this happiness is, and the masses do not give the same account of it as the philosophers. The former take it to be something clear and obvious such as pleasure, wealth, or fame. One man holds it to be this, and another that. Often the same man is of different minds at different times: After sickness it is health, and in poverty it is wealth. When they are impressed with the consciousness of their own ignorance, they admire most those who say grand things that are above their comprehension.

On the other hand, some philosophers have thought that, besides these particular good things, there is an "absolute" good {or Form of the Good}[5], which is the cause of whatever good there is in these particular good things.

As it would hardly be worthwhile to review all the opinions that have been held, we will confine ourselves to those that are most popular or seem to have some foundation in reason...

The "former" are the _____
_____.

1095a29

How did your definition of Aristotle's chief good compare with his definition?

Aristotle says the chief good is _____ and his

only reason thus far is _____.

Looking at both our definitions I would say _____

_____.

What does Aristotle mean when he says, "after sickness it is health, and in poverty it is wealth. When they are impressed with the consciousness of their ignorance, they admire most those who say grand things that are above their comprehension"?

The "it" he is referring to is _____.

The general point he is making about the masses is _____

_____.

Underline the various incorrect views of happiness in the next chapter.

5. What are other incorrect views of the chief good or happiness (which has been shown to be the same thing)?

1095b14

...As to men's notions of the good or happiness, it seems that the masses, to judge from their lives, hold it to be pleasure and so accept the life of pleasure as their ideal.

The three most well known kinds of life are: the life of pleasure, the life of the statesman, and the contemplative life.

The mass of men are completely slavish in their preference for the life of brute beasts, but their views must be considered because many of those in high places have the tastes of Sardanapalus.[6]

Cultivated and active men prefer honor because I suppose we may say that honor is the aim of the statesman's life. But this seems too superficial to be the good we are seeking, for honor appears to depend on those who give rather than those who receive it, while we have the feeling that the good is something that is uniquely a man's own and cannot easily be taken away from him.

The difference between honor and the good is that honor is _____

_____

_____

while the good is _____

_____

_____.

Moreover, these same men seem to pursue honor so that they can be assured of their own excellence. At least they wish to be honored by intelligent men and those who know them on the basis of their virtue or excellence. It is plain, then, that in their view virtue or excellence is better than honor; and perhaps we should take this to be the end of the statesman's life, rather than honor.

But virtue or excellence also cannot be the end we want, because it seems that a man might have virtue and yet be asleep or inactive all his life and might, moreover, meet with the greatest disasters and misfortunes. No one would maintain that such a man is happy, except for argument's sake. We will not dwell on those matters now, for they are sufficiently discussed in {my} popular treatises.

1096a

The third kind of life is the life of contemplation: We will discuss it further on.[7]

As for the money-making life, it lacks freedom and wealth. It is evidently not the good we search for because it is merely useful as a means to something else. Thus we might take pleasure, virtue, or excellence to be ends rather than wealth, for they are chosen on their own account. But it seems that not even they are the end, though much breath has been wasted in attempts to show that they are.

> Let us consider what Aristotle means by the end or chief good of life. Think again about ends and means. You pull weeds, not because pulling weeds is an end in itself, but to produce the end of a weedless lawn. A weedless lawn might be a means to the end of selling your house; selling your house might be a means to the end of retiring by the seashore; you might retire by the seashore so that you can pursue some hobby; and so forth. Each of these ends was *a* good but not *the* good, not the chief good that your whole life and every action are ultimately aimed at. But the question is, is there any end that is a not a means to something else? Is there an end of all ends? Aristotle would say that happiness is the end that we all strive for. We do not achieve happiness so that we can go on to something further. Happiness is the genuine end, the end of all our ends, the chief good. Now, write down some examples of means to ends with the final end being the equivalent of happiness.
>
> Studying this book carefully is a means to the end of _____ _____. But that would be the means to a still higher end of _____. And achieving that end, I would then use it as a means to the higher end of _____. And that might be the means to the end of happiness.
>
> Before Aristotle presents his own definition of happiness, he refutes Plato's doctrine of the Form of the Good. Aristotle agrees that the good is the end or goal of life; he just does not agree that this good is the Form of the Good. The following chapter is the most difficult in Book I. Reread, if you need to, the discussion in the Introduction about the difference between the Form of the Good for Plato and Aristotle's chief good.

6. What are the arguments against Plato's doctrine of the Form of the Good?

Dismissing those views, then, we must now consider the Form of the Good, and state the difficulties it presents; though such an inquiry is not a pleasant task because of our friendship with the author of the Doctrine of Ideas. But we believe that this is the right course, and that in the interests of truth we ought to sacrifice even what is nearest to us, especially as we call ourselves philosophers. Both are dear to us, but it is a sacred duty to give the preference to truth...[8]

The "author" Aristotle refers to is

_____.

1096a16

{The first and second refutations are omitted.}

Thirdly, since there is but one science of all the things that come under one idea, there would be but one science of all good things; but as it is, there are many sciences of good things; there are many sciences even of the goods that come under one category; for example, the science that deals with the correct or good timing in war is strategy, but the science that deals with the correct or good timing in curing disease is medicine. The science of the correct or good amount in regard to food is medicine, but the science that deals with the correct or good amount in regard to exercise is the science of gymnastics.

Underline Aristotles's key points in each of the following arguments.

One might ask what those who hold the Theory of Forms mean by the absolute. In *absolute man* and *man* the word *man* has one and the same sense because in regard to manhood there will be no difference between them. Thus, there will be no difference in regard to goodness between absolute good and good.

1096a33

1096b

Fifthly, they do not make the good any more good by making it eternal. A white thing that lasts a long time is no whiter than what lasts but a day....

Good, then, is not a term that is applied to all these things alike in the same sense or with reference to one common Idea or Form....

We can dismiss the further consideration of the Idea because even granting that this term *good*, which is applied to all these different things, has one and the same meaning throughout, or that there is an absolute good apart from these particulars, it is evident that this good will not be anything that man can realize or attain. But it is a good of this kind {that can be attained} that we are now seeking.

It might perhaps be thought that it would nevertheless be well to acquaint ourselves with this Form of the Good, with a view to the goods that are attainable and realizable. With this for a pattern, it may be said, we shall more readily know our own good and, knowing, achieve it.

1097a

There certainly is some plausibility in this argument, but it seems to be at variance with the existing sciences, because though they are all aiming at some good and striving to fill up their gaps {of knowledge}, they neglect to inquire about this form of the good. It is unlikely that the practitioners of the arts and sciences should not know or even look for what would help them so much.

The words "this argument" refer to

_____

_____

_____

_____.

Aristotle's point in this argument is

_____
_____
_____
_____
_____ .

I also wonder how the weaver or the carpenter would be aided in his craft by a knowledge of the Form of the Good, or how a man would be more able to heal the sick or command an army by contemplation of the pure form or idea. It seems to me that the physician does not seek for health in this abstract way but for the health of man—or rather of some particular man, for it is individuals that he has to heal.

Let me guide you through one of Aristotle's refutations of Plato's doctrine of the Form of the Good.

Aristotle says in his third refutation, "Thirdly, since there is but one science of all the things that come under one concept, there would be but one science of all good things...."

Aristotle is saying, that just as biology is the study of all kinds of life, we could reason that there would be a study of all kinds of goods (good food, good luck, good people), if there really was a Form of the Good. Since life has common characteristics we can study it under one science, biology. Because there is no "science of the good," there cannot be any common characteristics that all good things share, therefore there is no Form of the Good. Try putting this argument in your own words, but use a science other than biology.

You seem to be saying _____

_____

_____

_____ .

Then Aristotle says, "but as it is, there are many sciences of good things; there are many sciences even of the goods that come under one category. For example, the science that deals with the correct or good timing in war is strategy, but the science that deals with the correct or good timing in curing disease is medicine. The science of the correct or good amount in regard to food is medicine, but the science that deals with the correct or good amount in regard to exercise is the science of gymnastics."

In other words, Aristotle is describing several kinds of goods: the good or right opportunity (which are different things in war and medicine) and the good or right amount (which are different things in medicine and gymnastics). Here is a hard question. How is this observation part of his refutation of Plato?

Reading back over this short section and thinking through this very slowly I would have to say _____

_____ . Finally,

summing up some of Aristotle's main points in his refutation of Plato's Form of the Good _____

_____

_____ .

The next chapter is divided into two parts. Note that Aristotle now returns to his topic, the description of happiness.

7A. What is the chief good for mankind, and what arguments support this view?

Leaving these matters let us return once more to the question, what is the nature of the good we are seeking?

This good seems to be different in different kinds of action and in different arts—one thing in medicine, another in war, and so on. What then is the good in each of these cases? Surely it is that for the sake of which all else is done. In medicine the end is health, in war it is victory, in building it is a house—a different thing in each different case—but there is always, in whatever we do and in whatever we choose, an end. For it is always for the sake of the end that all else is done.

If then there be one end of all that man does, this end—or these ends, if there be more than one—will be the good attainable by action.[9]

Our argument has thus come round by a different path to the same point as before. {Chapter 2 above} This point we must try to explain more clearly.

We see that there are many ends. But some of these are chosen only as means, as wealth, flutes, and the whole class of instruments. So it is plain that not all ends are final. But the chief good must be something final. If there is only one final end, this will be what we are seeking—or if there are more than one, the most final of them.

Whatever is pursued as an end in itself is more final than whatever is pursued as means to something else. And whatever is never chosen as a means is more final than whatever is chosen both as an end in itself and as a means to another end. The strictly final end is the one that is always chosen as an end in itself and never as a means.

Happiness seems more than anything else to answer to this description, for we always choose happiness for itself and never for the sake of something else. On the other hand, we choose honor, pleasure, reason, and all virtue or excellence partly for themselves but partly also for the sake of happiness, because we believe that they will help make us happy. But no one chooses happiness for the sake of these things or as a means to anything else at all.

1097b

The reason no one chooses happiness as a means to another end is _____

_____

_____ .

The "conclusion" Aristotle refers to

is _____

_____

_____

We seem to be led to the same conclusion when we start from the notion of self-sufficiency.

The final good is thought to be self-sufficient. An example of the way we are using this term {*self-sufficient*} is that we do not regard a man as a solitary self, but we also take account of parents, children, wife, and, in short, friends and fellow citizens generally, since man is by nature a political being. Some limit must indeed be set to this, because if you go on to parents and descendants and friends of friends, you will never come to a stop. But this we will consider further on. For the present we will take self-sufficient to mean what by itself makes life desirable and lacking in nothing. Happiness is believed to answer this description.

Furthermore, happiness is believed to be the most desirable thing in the world and not merely one among other good things. If it were merely one among other good things (so that other things could be added to it), it is plain that the addition of the least of other goods must make it more desirable. The reason for this is that the addition would produce an extra amount of good and of two goods the greater is always more desirable.

Thus it seems that happiness is something final and self-sufficient and is the end of all that man does.

Pick two of the main points you underlined in this section, put them in your own words and give an original example of each.

I underlined "_____

_____

_____."

What Aristotle means is _____

_____

_____.

An example of this would be _____

_____

_____.

I also underlined "_____

_____

_____."

What Aristotle means is _____

_____.

An example of this would be _____
_____.

Try putting the following into your own words.

"Whatever is pursued as an end in itself is more final than whatever is pursued as means to something else. And whatever is never chosen as a means is more final than whatever is chosen both as an end in itself and as a means to another end. The strictly final end is the one that is always chosen as an end in itself and never as a means."

In the first sentence he is saying _____
_____.

For example, _____.

In the second sentence his point is _____
_____.

For example, _____.

In the third sentence _____
_____.

Aristotle's example of this is _____.

Here is another occasion to try to solve one of Aristotle's problems. He says that there is a final good, an end of all ends, for man, and then he points out that this must be happiness (and not honor, wealth, or even virtue). How would you define happiness? Remember that this has to be a perfect happiness to which, once we fully possessed it, nothing further could be added in our life. Also, remember that this must be a definition of happiness not just for you but for all humans.

True human happiness is _____
_____
_____.

Once a human possessed this, there would be no higher end to

life because _____
_____
_____.

This would be true for humans in general and not just myself

because _____
_____.

Now compare your answer with Aristotle's.

Underline Aristotle's answer to the question posed in the title to 7B.

1097b23

7B. What is happiness, and how does it relate to the function of man?

But perhaps the reader thinks that though no one will dispute the statement that happiness is the best thing in the world; nonetheless a still more precise definition of it is needed.

This will be achieved, I think, by asking: "What is the function of man?" Just as the goodness and the excellence of a flute player, or a sculptor, or any craftsman—and generally of those who have any special job or profession—lies in that function, so man's good seems to lie in his function, if he has one.

But can we suppose that, while a carpenter and a cobbler have functions and specialized activities of their own, man has no specialized activities and no function assigned him by nature? Surely as each part of his body—eye, hand, and foot—obviously has its own function, so we must suppose that man also has some function above all these.

What is it?

What man shares with plants is ___
_____ .

1098a

Man evidently has life in common even with the plants, but we want a characteristic that is peculiar to him. Therefore we must exclude the life of mere nutrition and growth.

Next to this comes the life of sense perception; but this too man plainly shares with horses and cattle and all kinds of animals.

There remains then the life whereby he acts—the life of his rational soul, with its two sides or divisions, one rational in that it obeys the rule of reason, the other rational as it actually possesses and exercises the power of reasoning....

What is unique about man is _____
_____
_____ .

The function of man, then, is an activity of the soul in conformity with reason, or at least not divided from reason....

Man's function being, as we say, a kind of life—that is to say, exercise of his soul in conformity with reason—the good man's function is to do this well and beautifully or nobly. And the function of anything is done well when it is done in accordance with the virtue of that thing. Putting all this together, then, we find that the good of man is an activity of his soul in accordance with virtue, or, if there be more than one, in accordance with the best and most complete virtue.

But there must also be a complete life span for this activity; for one swallow or one fine day does not make a spring, nor does one day or any small space of time make a blessed or happy man.

This may be taken as a rough outline of the good, because this, I think, is the proper method: first to sketch the outline and then to fill in the details. It seems that, once the outline is well done, anyone can carry on the work and fill in the items that time reveals to us or helps us to find. And indeed this is the way in which the arts and sciences have grown, because it requires no extraordinary genius to fill up the gaps.

However, we must bear in mind what was said above and not demand the same degree of accuracy in all branches of study, but in each case only as much as the subject matter allows and as is proper to that kind of inquiry. The carpenter and the geometer both look for the right angle, but in different ways. The former wants only the kind of approximation that his work requires, but the latter wants to know what constitutes a right angle, or what is its special quality. His aim is to find out the truth. And so in other cases we must follow the same course lest we spend more time on smaller points than the major task.

What was Aristotle's definition of happiness?

He said, "_____

_____." The essential difference

between his definition and mine is _____

_____.

Now think about the concept of function. What is the function tion of a hammer?

The function of a hammer is obviously to _____.
What is the function of a pen?

Obviously _____. And now you are going to ask what Aristotle says is the function of man. His answer is

_____.

In other words, from Aristotle's point of view, everything that exists has a special purpose, something that it is suited for better than any other thing. Just as the parts of man have a function (the eye to see, the ear to hear, and so forth) man as a whole must have some special function. Fulfilling this function, which man alone can do, would result in fulfillment or happiness. The function of man, as Aristotle pointed out, is "an activity of the soul in accordance with virtue." To live in accordance with virtue is to fulfill the unique potential of the human soul; nothing else in the universe has this potential. Of course, this raises a new question. What is virtue? Aristotle will give a lengthy account of this beginning in Book II. Make your own attempt to define virtue. Start with examples of virtuous actions and then show what the examples hold in common. (Think of it this way: If I asked you to define dessert and you presented the examples of apple pie, ice cream, and pineapple upside-down cake and then said that these all had in common the characteristics of being sweet, being eaten after a main meal, and adding large amounts of calories, that would be a beginning of a definition of dessert.)

Some examples of virtuous actions would be _____

_____

_____.

The characteristics these all have in common are _____

_____

_____.

This would be the beginning of my definition of virtue. Another example of virtue that fits this definition would be _____

because _____.

We will return to your definition later on the tour.

In the next chapter Aristotle shows how well-known views of happiness support his definition of happiness. This is an important test of the truth of ethical statements for Aristotle. Both Plato and Aristotle take the aristocratic position that the masses are generally foolish. Aristotle, however, takes the paradoxical view that even though the masses live foolishly, somehow the norms and popular opinions of society hold wisdom. Often in the *Nicomachean Ethics* he tests his conclusions to see how well they accord with what is generally believed to be true.

Toward the end of the following chapter, Aristotle considers whether material possessions are necessary to happiness. What do you think he will say, and what is your view?

I believe he will say _____

_____

_____

_____

_____.

My view is _____

_____

_____

_____

_____.

Underline answers to the title question and information about Aristotle's view of possessions.

8. What other current views support this account of happiness?

We must not be satisfied, then, with examining this starting point or principle of ours as a conclusion from our data but must also view it in its relation to current opinions on the subject. All facts harmonize with a true principle, but a false one is soon found to be incompatible with the facts....

Our account {of happiness}, again, is in harmony with the common saying that the happy man lives well and does well because we may say that happiness, according to us, is living well and doing well.

And, indeed, all the characteristics that men expect to find in happiness, seem to belong to happiness as we define it.

Some hold it to be virtue or excellence, some prudence, others a kind of wisdom; others, again, hold it to be all or some of these, with the addition of pleasure, either as an ingredient or as a necessary accompaniment; and some even include external prosperity in their account of it.

Now some of these views have the support of many voices and of traditional authorities; others have few voices, but those are held in high prestige. It is probable that neither one side nor the other is entirely wrong but that in some one point at least, if not in most, they are both right.

First, then, the view that happiness is virtue or a kind of virtue harmonizes with our account because "actions of the soul in conformity with virtue" belong to virtue.

But I think we may say that it makes no small difference whether the good is conceived as the mere possession of something or as its use—as a disposition, or as the exercise of that disposition. For the disposition may be present and yet produce no good result, as when a man is asleep or in any other way hindered from his function; but with its exercise this is not possible for it must show itself in acts and in good acts. Just as at the Olympic games it is not the fairest and strongest who receive the crown but those who contend, for among these are the victors, in life the winners are those who not only have all the virtues but also act on them.

Furthermore, the life of these men is in itself pleasant because pleasure belongs to the soul, and each man takes pleasure in what he is said to love—he who loves horses in horses, he who loves theater in plays. In the same way he who loves justice takes pleasure in acts of justice, and generally the lover of excellence or virtue takes pleasure in virtuous acts....

And while with most men there is a perpetual conflict among the many things in which they find pleasure, since these are not naturally pleasant, those who love what is noble take pleasure in that which is naturally pleasant....

1098b9

What Aristotle is going to do in this chapter is _____

_____

_____

because _____

_____ .

1099a

The comparison Aristotle makes between successful Olympic athletes and virtuous individuals is

that both  _____

_____

_____

_____ .

Their life {those who do virtuous acts}, then, does not need pleasure to be added to it as an appendage but contains pleasure in itself.

Indeed, in addition to what we have said, a man is not good at all unless he takes pleasure in noble deeds. No one would call a man just who did not take pleasure in doing justice nor generous who took no pleasure in acts of generosity, and so on.

If this be so, the actions performed in conformity with virtue will be pleasant in themselves. But they are also both good and noble in the highest degree, at least if the man of good character's judgment about them is right....

Happiness, then, is the best and noblest and pleasantest thing in the world, and these are not separated, as the Delian inscription[10] would have them be:

> What is most just is noblest, health is best,
> Pleasantest is to get your heart's desire.

For all these characteristics are united in the best activities of our soul, and these, or some one of them that is better than all the others, we identify with happiness.

Nevertheless, happiness plainly requires external goods because it is impossible, or at least not easy, to act nobly without some material goods. There are many things that can only be done through instruments, so to speak, such as friends, and wealth, and political influence. There are some things whose absence takes the bloom from our happiness, as good birth, the blessing of children, personal beauty. A man is not likely to be happy if he is very ugly, or of low birth, or alone in the world, or childless, and perhaps still less if he has worthless children or friends or has lost good ones that he had.

As we said, then, happiness seems to stand in need of this kind of prosperity, and so some identify it with good fortune, just as others identify it with virtue.

1099b
Aristotle's point in this paragraph is
_____
_____
_____
_____
_____
_____.

Here is an interesting problem to try to solve before you begin reading the next chapter. Aristotle's definition of happiness is "an activity of the soul in conformity with virtue." Under this definition, could an animal be called happy? Could a child?

Thinking about whether or not an animal could be happy, I personally would say _____
_____ because _____
_____.

Aristotle, according to his definition, would probably say _____
_____.

About a child he would say _____

_____ because _____

_____. My own view is _____

_____. Two pieces of evidence to support

my view are first _____

_____ and second _____

_____.

Now see what Aristotle says.

9. Is happiness acquired or a gift of the gods or of chance?

This has led people to ask whether happiness is acquired by learning, the formation of habits, or any other kind of training or comes by some divine gift or even by chance.

Well, if the gods do give gifts to men, happiness is likely to be among these gifts, more likely than anything else, in proportion as it is better than all other human things.

This belongs more properly to another branch of inquiry, but we may say that even if happiness is not a gift of the gods, but comes as a consequence of virtue or some kind of learning or training, it still seems to be one of the most divine things in the world because the crown and end of virtue appears to be better than anything else and something divine and blessed.

Again, if it is thus acquired, it will be widely accessible because it will then be in the power of all, except those who have lost the capacity for virtue, to acquire it by study and diligence.

And if it is better that men should attain happiness in this way rather than by chance, it is reasonable to suppose that it is so, since in the realm of nature all things are arranged in the best possible way. This is also true in the realm of art, and of any kind of causation, and most of all in the realm of the highest kind of causation. Indeed it would be too absurd to leave what is highest and fairest to the mercy of chance.

But our definition itself clears up the difficulty because happiness was defined as a certain kind of activity of the soul in accordance with virtue. Of the remaining goods, other than happiness itself, some must be present as necessary prerequisites, while others are aids and useful instruments to happiness. This agrees with what we said at the beginning. We then established that the end of the science of politics is the best of all ends, but the chief purpose of that science is to make citizens of a certain character, that is, good and

The words "this way" refer to _____

_____

_____.

disposed to perform virtuous actions. It is not without reason, then, that we do not call an ox, or a horse, or any brute happy because none of them is able to share in this kind of activity.

For the same reason also a child is not happy; he is as yet, because of his age, unable to perform such things {i.e., activities of the soul in conformity with virtue}. If we ever call a child happy, it is because we hope he has promise of doing them in the future. For, as we said, happiness requires not only perfect excellence or virtue but also a full term of years for its exercise. Our life is liable to many changes and to all sorts of chances, and it is possible that he who is most prosperous now will in his old age meet with great disasters, as is told of Priam in the tales of the heroes. A man who thus encounters such blows of fate and comes to a miserable end cannot be called happy.

What was Aristotle's reasoning in regard to the happiness of animals and children?

He says "_____

_____." His point is

_____.

It is now time to review. Look back at your notes and then succinctly answer each of these chapter title questions.

1. What do all human actions aim at?

_____

_____

_____.

2. What science studies the chief good?

_____

_____

_____.

3. Why can't the investigation of politics be exact?

_____

_____

_____.

4. What is the chief good, and what are some of the views about it?

_____

_____

_____.

5. What are other incorrect views of the chief good or happiness (which has been shown to be the same thing)?

_____

_____

_____ .

6. What are the arguments against Plato's doctrine of the Form of the Good? (Try to state the one we went through together.)

_____

_____

_____

_____

_____ .

7A. What is the chief good for mankind, and what arguments support this view?

_____

_____

_____ .

7B. What is happiness, and how does it relate to the function of man?

_____

_____

_____ .

8. What other current views support this account of happiness?

_____

_____

_____ .

9. Is happiness acquired or a gift of the gods or of chance?

_____

_____

_____ .

The next chapter begins a new topic. Aristotle did not arrange his manuscript into books and chapters, that was done by editors many years after he died. You will see that the next chapter probably would be better placed at the beginning of Book II.

13. What are the parts of the soul?

1102a5

Underline in this and future chapters Aristotle's answer to the question posed in the chapter title.

Since happiness is an activity of the soul in conformity with perfect virtue, we will now inquire about what virtue is. This will probably help us in our inquiry about happiness.

Indeed the true statesman seems to be especially concerned with virtue, for he wishes to make the citizens good and obedient to the laws. Of this we have an example in the Cretan and the Lacedaemonian lawgivers, and any others who resembled them. Thus, if the inquiry belongs to politics or the science of the state, it is plain that it will be in accordance with our original purpose to pursue it. The virtue or excellence that we are to consider is, of course, the excellence of man because it is the good of man and the happiness of man that we started to seek. By the excellence of man I mean excellence not of body but of soul, because happiness we take to be an activity of the soul. If this is so, it is evident that the statesman must have some knowledge of the soul, just as the man who is to heal the eye or the whole body must have some knowledge of each. This is even truer for the statesman than for the doctor because the science of politics is better and more valuable than the science of medicine....

As statesmen or students of politics, then, we must inquire into the nature of the soul, but in so doing we must keep our special purpose in view and go only as far as that requires. To go into greater detail would be too laborious for the present undertaking.

There are certain points that are stated with sufficient precision even in our popular accounts of the soul, and these we will adopt here. The soul is presented {in these accounts} as having two parts, a rational and an irrational.

Whether these are separated as are the parts of the body or any divisible thing, or whether they are only distinguishable in thought, but in fact inseparable, like concave and convex in the circumference of a circle, makes no difference for our present purpose.

Of the irrational part, then, one part seems to be common to all things that live, and to be possessed by plants. I mean that which causes nutrition and growth because we must assume that all things that take nourishment have a capacity of this kind, even when they are embryos, and have the same capacity when they are full grown; at least this is more reasonable than to suppose that they have a different one then.

1102b

The words "this part" refer back to

_____

_____

_____.

The excellence of this part of the soul, then, is plainly not specifically human but one that man shares with other beings. This is confirmed by the fact that this nutritive part of the soul is thought to be most active in sleep, because the distinction between the good and the bad man shows itself least in sleep. This is the source of the saying that for half their lives there is no difference between the happy and the miserable. This is what we should expect; for sleep

34   BOOK I

is the cessation of the soul from those functions that cause it to be called good or bad, except when the motions of the body make their way in and give occasion to dreams, which are better in the good man than in ordinary people. However, we need not pursue this further, and may dismiss the nutritive principle {in the soul} since it has no place in the virtue or excellence of man.

However, there seems to be another vital principle that is irrational and yet in some way partakes of reason. In the morally strong and the morally weak man alike we praise the reason or the rational part, for it exhorts them correctly and urges them to do what is best; but there is plainly present in them another principle besides the rational one, which fights and struggles against the reason. Just as a paralyzed limb, when you will to move it to the right, moves on the contrary to the left, so it is with the soul; the morally weak man's impulses run counter to his reason. But while we see the disobedient member in the case of the body, we do not see it in the case of the soul. We must nevertheless hold that in the soul, too, there is something beside the reason, which opposes and runs counter to it, though in what sense it is distinct from the reason does not matter here.

This part seems, however, to partake of reason also, as we said: At least in the morally strong man it submits to reason. In the self-controlled and courageous man we may say it is still more obedient because in him it is altogether in harmony with the reason.

It appears that the irrational part, then, is twofold. There is the nutritive faculty, which has no share of reason, and the faculty of appetite or of desire in general, which partakes of reason insofar as it listens to reason and submits to its sway. When we say "partakes of reason" or "listens to reason," we mean this in the sense in which we talk of "listening to reason" from parents or friends, not in the sense in which we talk of listening to the reasonings of mathematicians.

Furthermore, all advice, rebuke, and exhortation testify that the irrational part is in some way amenable to reason.

If we say that this part, too, has a share of reason, the rational part will also have two divisions: one rational in the strict sense as possessing reason in itself, the other rational as listening to reason as a man listens to his father.

On this division of the faculties {of the soul} is based the division of virtue, for we speak of intellectual virtues and of moral virtues; theoretical wisdom and intelligence and practical wisdom we call intellectual virtues, generosity and self-control we call moral virtues. When we are speaking of a man's moral character we do not say that he is wise or intelligent but that he is gentle or self-controlled. But we praise the wise man, too, for his habit of mind or characteristics that are praiseworthy in what we call an excellence or virtue.

The reason the "nutritive principle" has "no place in the virtue or excellence of man" is _____ _____ _____ _____ _____.

1103a

Reread this chapter and place a labeled diagram of the soul in the space above.

Look back at the last paragraphs and try to answer the question, What are the two major parts of the soul, and how is each of these parts divided?

The two parts of the soul are the _____ and the

_____ . The former is divided into _____

_____ and _____ . The

latter is divided into _____

and _____ .

And what are the two kinds of virtues?

Aristotle says one kind is _____ .

The other kind is _____ .

In the first chapter of Book II Aristotle considers the problem of the origin of intellectual and moral virtue. First of all, what are some examples of each?

Examples of intellectual virtue offered by Aristotle are

_____ .

Perhaps one could also add _____

_____ . Aristotle's examples of moral virtue are

_____ .

Other moral virtues might be _____

_____ .

The question now is, Where do these virtues come from? Do we become intellectual and/or morally virtuous as a result of habit or learning, or are these virtues with us at birth (inborn) or are they a gift of the gods?

Do both intellectual and moral virtues have the same origin or different origins? Pause for a few moments now, think about the examples above and then give your wisest answers.

Intellectual virtues like _____

probably come from _____

because _____

_____ .

Moral virtues like _____ probably

come from _____ because

_____ .

Now, let us see what Aristotle says.

BOOK II
Moral Virtue

1. How is moral virtue acquired?

Virtue, then, being of these two kinds, intellectual and moral, intellectual virtue owes its birth and growth mainly to instruction and so requires time and experience, while moral virtue, *ethike*, is the result of habit, *ethos*, and has accordingly in our language received a name formed by a slight change from *ethos*.[11]

1103a14

From this it is plain that none of the moral virtues is implanted in us by nature, because what is implanted by nature cannot be altered by training. For example, a stone by nature tends to fall downward, and you could not train it to rise upward, though you tried to do so by throwing it up ten thousand times, nor could you train fire to move downward, nor accustom anything that by nature behaves in one way to behave in any other way.

The virtues, then, come neither by nature nor against nature, but nature gives the capacity for acquiring them, and this is developed by training.

Put this short paragraph into your own words. Aristotle is saying,

_____

_____

_____

_____

_____.

Again, where we do things by nature we have the power to use them before we do in fact use them. We plainly see this in the case of the senses, because it is not by constantly seeing and hearing that we acquire those faculties; we had the power first and then used it, instead of acquiring the power by the use. But the virtues we acquire by doing the acts, as is the case with the arts. We learn an art by doing what we wish to do when we have learned it; we become builders by building and harpers by harping. And so by doing just acts we become just, and by doing acts of self-control and courage we become self-controlled and courageous. This is also attested by what occurs in states, because the legislators make their

1103b

citizens good by training; at least this is the wish of all legislators, and those who do not succeed in this miss their aim. It is this that distinguishes a good from a bad constitution.

Again, both the moral virtues and the corresponding vices result from and are formed by the same acts, and that is also the case with the arts. It is by harping that good harpers and bad harpers alike are produced. And so it is with builders and the rest; by building well they become good builders, and by building badly they become bad builders. If it were not so, they would not have anybody to teach them but would all be born either good or bad at their trades. And it is just the same with the virtues. It is by acting justly or unjustly in our relations with other men that we become just or unjust, and by acting in dangerous circumstances and training ourselves to feel confidence or fear that we become courageous or cowardly. It is the same with our animal appetites and our feelings of anger, because by behaving in this way or that on the occasions when these passions are aroused, some become self-controlled and gentle and others self-indulgent and short-tempered. In essence, acts of any kind produce habits or characters of the same kind.

Hence we ought to make sure that our acts are of a certain kind because the resulting character changes as they change. It makes no small difference, therefore, whether a man is trained from his youth up in this way or in that, but a great difference, or rather all the difference.

If someone said people are born either good or bad, Aristotle would

reply, _____
_____
_____
_____
_____
_____.

In the second paragraph Aristotle says, "it is plain that none of the moral virtues is implanted in us by nature, because what is implanted by nature cannot be altered by training. For example, a stone by nature tends to fall downward, and you could not train it to rise upward, though you tried to do so by throwing it up ten thousand times, nor could you train fire to move downward, nor accustom anything that by nature behaves in one way to behave in any other way."

When he says that virtues are not "implanted in us by nature" he means that our virtues are not innate, inborn. We are not born courageous or self-controlled. But if we are not born this way, where does our courage or self-control come from, and what does this have to do with trying to train stones?

Aristotle is making the point about the relationship between

moral virtues and the training of stones that _____
_____
_____.

Thus, the contrast he is making between a stone falling downward and a human acting courageously is _____

_____

_____.

In the next paragraphs in the chapter he describes how we acquire virtue. He says, "_____

_____

_____. His point is

_____

_____.

    Do you think he is right?

    Consider this example. One of the most courageous persons
I can think of would be _____. A specific
courageous act by this person would be _____

_____.

When I ask myself if this virtue of courage was inborn or not, I
must say _____

_____ because _____

_____. Other

evidence in support of my view would be _____

_____.

What I am saying in relation to Aristotle is _____

_____.

    After you finish reading the following chapter, return and
write in your own chapter title. It should sum up the general
topic of Chapter 2.

2.

But our present inquiry has not, like the rest, a merely speculative
aim. We are not inquiring merely to know what excellence or virtue
is, but to become good. Otherwise it would profit us nothing. We
must ask therefore about these acts and see what kind they are
because, as we said, they determine our character.

    First of all, it is a common characteristic of them that they must
be in accordance with right reason, which we shall here take for
granted, reserving for future discussion[12] the question what this
right reason is and how it is related to the other virtues.

    But let it be understood that all reasoning on matters of practice
must be in outline merely and not scientifically exact, for, as we said
at the beginning, the kind of reasoning to be demanded varies with

The word "them" refers to _____

_____.

1104a

the subject at hand. In practical matters and questions of what is beneficial there are no invariable laws, any more than there are in questions of health.

If our general conclusions are inexact, still more inexact is all reasoning about particular cases, because these fall under no system of scientifically established rules or traditional maxims, but the individual must always consider for himself what the special occasion requires, just as in medicine or navigation. But although this is the case, we must try to provide what help we can.

First of all, we must observe that in matters of this sort moral qualities are destroyed by deficiency and excess. This is obvious. For example, to illustrate what we cannot see by what we can see, in the case of strength and health too much and too little exercise alike destroy strength. To take too much meat and drink and to take too little are equally ruinous to health, but the proper amount produces, increases, and preserves it. It is the same with self-control, courage, and the other virtues. The man who shuns and fears everything and never makes a stand becomes a coward, while the man who fears nothing at all but will face anything becomes foolhardy. So, too, the man who takes his fill of any kind of pleasure and abstains from none is self-indulgent, but the man who shuns all like a boor might be called extremely inhibited.[13] Self-control and courage are destroyed by both excess and deficiency but preserved by the mean.

Habits or types of character are not only produced, preserved, and destroyed by the same occasions and the same actions but will also show themselves in the same circumstances. This is the case with visible things like strength. Strength is produced by taking plenty of nourishment and doing a great deal of hard work, and the strong man, in turn, has the greatest capacity for these. The case is the same with the virtues: By abstaining from excessive pleasure we become self-controlled, and when we have become self-controlled we are best able to abstain. And so with courage: By habituating ourselves to despise danger and to face it, we become courageous; when we have become courageous, we are best able to face danger.

Another example of excess and deficiency might be the excess of

_____

_____

and the deficiency of _____

_____.
The mean between these two would

be _____

_____.

1104b

1104b4

First go back and write in your chapter title, then think about the following sentence. "For self-control and courage are destroyed by both excess and deficiency but preserved by the mean."

Aristotle is saying _____

_____. The examples he gave

to illustrate this are _____

_____. Take

another example, saving money. The "excess" would make one

a _____ and the "deficiency" would make one

_____. Thus, Aristotle's point in general

is that _____

_____.

At the end of the chapter Aristotle says, "And the case is the same with the virtues: By abstaining from excessive pleasure we become self-controlled, and when we have become self-controlled we are best able to abstain. And so with courage: By habituating ourselves to despise danger and to face it, we become courageous; when we have become courageous, we are best able to face danger."
What does he mean?

He means _____

_____.

For example, _____

_____.

Read the first two paragraphs of Chapter 4 closely. The first paragraph states an argument that Aristotle refutes in the second.

4.   How does one become virtuous?

But here we may be asked what we mean by saying that men can become just and self-controlled only by doing what is just and self-controlled. Surely, it may be said, if their acts are just and self-controlled, they themselves are already just and self-controlled, as they are grammarians and musicians if they do what is grammatical and musical.

We may answer, I think, firstly that this is not quite the case even with the arts. A man may do something grammatical or write something correctly by chance, or at the prompting of another person. He will not be grammatical until he not only does something grammatical but also does it grammatically or like a grammatical person, that is, as a result of his own knowledge of grammar.

Secondly the virtues are not analogous to the arts. The products of art have their excellence in themselves, and so it is enough if when produced they are of a certain quality. In the case of the virtues a man is not said to act justly or temperately if he simply performs a just or temperate action; he must also be in a certain state of mind when he does it. That is, first he must know what he is doing; secondly he must choose it, and choose it for itself; and

1105a17
The argument in the first paragraph

is _____

_____

_____.

The refutation in the second

paragraph is _____

_____

_____

_____.

1105b

thirdly his act must be expression of a formed and stable character. Only one of these conditions, the knowledge, is necessary for the possession of any art; but for the possession of the virtues, knowledge is of little or no avail, while the other conditions that result from repeatedly doing what is just and self-controlled are not a little important but all-important.

The thing that is done, therefore, is called just or self-controlled when it is the same as the just or self-controlled man would do; but the man who does it is not just or self-controlled unless he also does it in the spirit of the just or the self-controlled man.

It is right, then, to say that a man becomes just by doing what is just and self-controlled by doing what is self-controlled, while without performing these actions he has no chance of ever becoming virtuous.

But most men, instead of performing such actions, play with theories and fancy that they are philosophizing and that this will make them good, like a sick man who listens attentively to what the doctor says and then disobeys all his orders. This sort of philosophizing will no more bring health to the soul than this sort of treatment will bring health to the body.

An example of becoming "just by doing what is just" would be the just action of _____ _____

which would make one just because _____ _____ _____ _____ _____.

Look back at the first two paragraphs. Aristotle is employing a classic philosophical strategy. In the first paragraph he presents a good objection to something he has previously demonstrated. In the second paragraph he refutes his own attempted refutation. A good argument involves not only the presentation of evidence but also the construction of strong arguments against that evidence. By refuting these strong arguments the original argument becomes even more persuasive.

In the first paragraph Aristotle is offering an objection to his previous argument that _____ _____. In essence, he is saying in the first paragraph _____ _____.

He answers this objection in the second paragraph by pointing out _____ _____.

Try this yourself.

Let us say I was attempting to argue that obedience to God was the highest ethical virtue. The major points in my argument would be _____

42   BOOK II

_____

_____.

The strongest possible objection I could make against this argument would be _____

_____

_____.

However, I can show this is not true because _____

_____

_____.

    Here is a problem that will help you understand part of the next chapter. The main task in Chapter 4 will be to show where the virtues are in the soul. According to Aristotle the soul (or mind; the two are synonymous for Aristotle and other Greeks) contains feelings, capacities, and dispositions. In essence he argues in the next chapter that because the virtues are neither feelings nor capacities, they must be dispositions. Try now to distinguish between feelings and virtues. Some examples of feelings are anger, fear, confidence, envy, and joy. Some examples of virtues are courage and self-control. Aristotle is able to offer four reasons why virtues are not the same thing as feelings.

    I would have to define virtues first then feelings and then try to show why the former could not be the later. Very well. Thinking about my previous definition of virtue on page _____, I could improve this by saying virtue would be _____

_____.

A definition of feelings that would include the ones listed above would be _____

_____.

Therefore, one reason a virtue could not be a feeling is _____

_____.

Another reason would be _____

_____.

For example, the difference between a feeling like envy and a virtue like courage would be _____

_____.

Now let's see what Aristotle has to say.

5. What genus or class does virtue belong to?

We next have to inquire what virtue is.

There are three things found in the soul: (1) feelings, (2) capacities, and (3) dispositions; virtue must be one of these three. By *feelings* we mean appetite, anger, fear, confidence, envy, joy, love, hate, longing, emulation, pity, or, generally, whatever is accompanied by pleasure or pain. By *capacities* we mean whatever allows us to be affected in any of these ways, such as anything that allows us to be angered or pained or to pity. By *disposition* we mean the condition, either good or bad, that we take in relation to our feelings; for example, in regard to being angered, we are in a bad disposition if we become excessively or insufficiently angry and in a good disposition if we feel the proper amount of anger. And so with the rest of our feelings.

Now the virtues are not feelings, nor are the vices: (1) because we are not called good or bad on the basis of our feelings but are called so on the basis of our virtues or vices; (2) because we are neither praised nor blamed on the basis of our feelings (a man is not praised for being afraid or angry or blamed for being angry simply, but for being angry in a particular way), but we are praised or blamed for our virtues or vices; (3) because we may be angered or frightened without deliberate choice, but the virtues are a kind of deliberate choice or at least are impossible without it; and (4) because with regard to our feelings we are said to be moved, but in regard to our virtues and vices we are not said to be moved but to be disposed in a particular way.

For these same reasons virtues and vices are not capacities because we are not called either good or bad for merely having a capacity for emotion, nor are we either praised or blamed for this. Furthermore, while nature gives us our capacities, nature does not make us either good or bad. This point, however, we have already discussed.

If, then, the virtues are neither feelings nor capacities, it only remains for them to be dispositions.

Feelings are _____
_____
_____.

Capacities are _____
_____
_____.

Dispositions are _____
_____
_____.

Of these three, virtues are in the class of _____
_____.

1106a

Look back at the four reasons Aristotle offered for saying feelings are not virtues. Put each in your own words.

The first reason why feelings are not virtues is _____
_____.

The second reason is _____
_____.

The third reason is _____

_____.

The fourth reason is _____

_____.

In the next chapter Aristotle offers a more precise definition of virtue.

6. How can virtue be more precisely defined?

We have thus found the genus to which virtue belongs, but we want to know not only that it is a disposition but also what species[14] of disposition it is.

Virtue is in the genus of _____

_____.

We may safely say that the virtue or excellence of a thing causes that particular thing to be in good condition and to perform its function well. The virtue or excellence of the eye, for instance, makes both the eye and its function good because it is by the excellence of the eye that we see well. So the proper excellence or virtue of the horse makes a horse what he should be and makes him good at running, carrying his rider, and mounting a charge.

If this holds true in all cases, the proper excellence or virtue of man will be a disposition that makes a man good and makes him perform his function well.

How this is to be done we have already said, but we may present the same conclusion in another way, by inquiring what the nature of this virtue is.

If we have any quantity, whether continuous or divisible into parts, it is possible to take either a larger, a smaller, or an equal amount, and this is true either in relation to the quantity or in relation to ourselves.

By an equal amount I understand an intermediate amount, or one that lies between excess and deficiency.

By the absolute intermediate or intermediate relative to the thing itself, I mean what is equidistant from both extremes, and this is the same for everyone. By the intermediate relative to us I mean what is neither too much nor too little for us; and this is not the same for everyone.

For example, if ten be too large and two be too small, six is the intermediate relative to the thing itself or the arithmetical intermediate, because if it is in the same relation to both extremes it is the intermediate in arithmetical proportion.

But the intermediate relative to us cannot be found in this way. If ten pounds of food is too much for a given man to eat, and two pounds is too little, it does not follow that the trainer will order him to eat six pounds: That also may perhaps be too much or too little for the man in question; too little for Milo {a champion wrestler},

1106b
Aristotle's point in this paragraph is

_____

_____.

too much for the beginner. The same holds true in running and wrestling.

And so we may say generally that the expert in any field avoids what is too much and what is too little, and seeks for the intermediate and chooses it—not the absolute but the intermediate relative to us.

Every art or science perfects its work in this way, looking to the intermediate and bringing its work up to this standard; so that people say of a good work that nothing could be taken from it or added to it, which implies that excellence is destroyed by excess or deficiency but secured by observing the mean. And good artists do in fact keep their eyes fixed on this in all that they do. Virtue therefore, since it is like nature and is more exact and better than any art, must also aim at the intermediate. By virtue, of course, I mean moral virtue because it has to do with passions and actions, and it is these that admit of excess and deficiency and the intermediate. For example, it is possible to feel fear, confidence, desire, anger, and pity and generally to be affected pleasantly and painfully, either too much or too little and in either case wrongly; but to be thus affected at the right times, on the right occasions, toward the right persons, with the right object, and in the right fashion is the intermediate and best course, and these are characteristics of virtue. In the same way our actions are characterized by excess, deficiency, and the intermediate or proper amount.

An example of a moral virtue might be

_____

_____.

Its "excess" would be _____

_____

because_____

_____

_____.

Its "deficiency" would be _____

_____

because_____.

1107a

Virtue, then, is involved with passions and with actions, in which excess and deficiency are wrong but the intermediate amount is praised and is right, both of which are characteristics of virtue. Virtue, then, is a kind of mean, inasmuch as it aims at the intermediate or moderate amount.

Again, there are many ways of going wrong (for evil is infinite in nature, to use Pythagorean terminology, while good is finite) but only one way of going right; so that the one is easy and the other hard—easy to miss the mark and hard to hit it. For this reason also excess and deficiency are characteristic of vice, hitting the mean is characteristic of virtue.

Goodness is simple, badness takes many shapes.

Virtue, then, is a disposition involving choice, the characteristic of which lies in moderation or observance of the mean relatively to the persons concerned, as determined by reason, that is, as the man of practical wisdom would determine it.

And virtue is a moderation, firstly because it comes in the middle or mean between two vices—one on the side of excess, the other on the side of deficiency. Secondly, it is a moderation inasmuch as, while the vices fall short of or exceed the proper amount in feeling and in action, virtue finds and chooses the intermediate.

Regarded in its essence, therefore, or according to the definition of its nature, virtue is a moderation or middle state, but viewed in its relation to what is best and right it is an extreme of perfection.

But not all actions or passions can be moderated. There are some whose very names imply evil, for example malice, shamelessness, and envy, and, among acts, adultery, theft, and murder. These and all other similar things are blamed because they are bad in themselves and not merely in their excess or deficiency. It is impossible therefore to go right in them; they are always wrong. Rightness and wrongness in such things, for example adultery, does not depend on whether it is the right person, occasion, and manner, but the mere doing of any of them is wrong.

It would be equally absurd to look for moderation, excess, or deficiency in unjust, cowardly, or self-indulgent conduct because then there would be moderation in excess or deficiency, and excess in excess, and deficiency in deficiency.

The fact is that just as there can be no excess or deficiency in self-control or courage because the intermediate or moderate amount is, in a sense, an extreme, so in those kinds of conduct also there can be no moderation, excess, or deficiency, but the acts are wrong however they are done. To put it generally, there cannot be moderation in excess or deficiency, or excess or deficiency in moderation.

In this chapter Aristotle expands one of the key ethical ideas of the *Nicomachean Ethics,* the concept of virtue as a mean between two extremes. Right action is the midpath between too much and too little. Obviously, this idea is still with us today. Think of your own examples of virtuous action between two vices, one a "deficiency" and the other an "excess."

This is fairly simple. Someone who ate too much would be _____. Someone who ate too little would be _____. The virtue in this case would be _____. One can exercise too much; such a person might be called _____. Or one can exercise too little; that person would be called _____. The mean between these vices of excess and deficiency would be _____. Studying too much would make one _____. Studying too little would make one _____. I, however, who study just the right amount, could be called _____. Other examples of the mean and excessive and deficient actions would be _____

_____

_____.

Reread the last two paragraphs. "(A) It would be equally absurd to look for moderation, excess, or deficiency in unjust, cowardly, or self-indulgent conduct because then there would be moderation in excess or deficiency, and excess in excess, and deficiency in deficiency.

"(B) The fact is that just as there can be no excess or deficiency in self-control or courage because the intermediate or moderate amount is, in a sense, an extreme, (C) so in those kinds of conduct also there can be no moderation, excess, or deficiency, but the acts are wrong however they are done. (D) To put it generally, there cannot be moderation in excess or deficiency, or excess or deficiency in moderation."

What do you think Aristotle means when he says there would be no "moderation in excess or deficiency, and excess in excess, and deficiency in deficiency"?

Well, I think, _____

_____.

What is he saying in (B)?

The point he is making is _____

_____.

How does he extend this idea in (C)?

_____

_____.

Read (D) now and explain why there can't "be moderation in excess or deficiency, or excess or deficiency in moderation."

Take adultery as an example of excess. If there were moderation in adultery, _____.

This would be absurd because _____

_____. Now take miserliness as an example of deficiency. If there were moderation in this deficiency, _____

_____. Therefore, _____

_____.

Next take the case of courage, which would be a mean between

_____ and _____. If there

could be a deficiency or excess of this moderation then _____

_____. Therefore, _____

_____.

Aristotle's general point is _____

_____.

    Now try to continue to think like Aristotle. Think of the two vices, one of excess and the other of deficiency, that correspond to the following means: courage (use the two you presented above if you wish), self-control, generosity, wittiness, and friendliness.

    If courage is the mean, the vice of deficiency would be

_____ and the vice of excess would be

_____. I will describe each of the others in

the same pattern. _____

_____

_____

_____

_____

_____.

    In the next chapter underline each of Aristotle's examples of the virtuous mean and its twin vices. Put a star by each one you analyzed in the same way as Aristotle.

7.   What are some examples of virtues and vices?

It is not enough to make these general statements about virtue and vice: We must go on and apply them to particular virtues and vices. In reasoning about matters of conduct general statements are too vague, and do not convey as much truth as particular propositions. It is with particulars that conduct is concerned. Our statements, therefore, when applied to these particulars, should be found to hold good….

    Moderation in the feelings of fear and confidence is courage: Of feelings that are excessive, he that exceeds in fearlessness has no name as often happens, but he that exceeds in confidence is foolhardy, while he that exceeds in fear, but is deficient in confidence, is cowardly.

    Moderation in regard to pleasures and also, though to a lesser extent, pains is self-control, while excess is self-indulgence. But

Underline Aristotle's examples.

1107b

Number each of the virtues on this and the following page.

deficiency in regard to these pleasures is hardly ever found, and so these sorts of people also have as yet received no name: Let us describe them as "empty of feeling."

In regard to giving and taking money, moderation is generosity and excess and deficiency are extravagance and stinginess. But these two vices exceed and fall short in opposite ways. The extravagant man exceeds in spending, but falls short in taking; while the stingy man exceeds in taking, but falls short in spending.

For the present we are giving only an outline or summary, and aim at nothing more; we shall afterwards describe these points in greater detail.

But there are other dispositions in regard to money: There is a moderation that is called magnificence (for the magnificent is not the same as the generous man since the former deals with large sums and the latter with small), an excess that is called bad taste or vulgarity, and a deficiency that is called miserliness. These vices differ from those that are opposed to generosity. How they differ will be explained later.

With respect to honor and disgrace, there is a moderation that is called great-souled,[15] an excess that may be called vanity, and a deficiency that may be called small-souled.[16]

But just as we said that generosity is related to magnificence, differing only in that it deals with small sums, here there is a virtue related to the great-souled, and differing only in that it is concerned with small instead of great honors. A man may have a proper desire for honor and also more or less than a proper desire. He that carries this desire to excess is called overly ambitious, he that has not enough of it is called unambitious, but he that has the proper amount has no name. There are also no abstract terms for corresponding dispositions, except *ambition,* corresponding to *ambitious.* And because of this, those who occupy the extremes lay claim to the middle place. In common parlance, too, the moderate man is sometimes called ambitious and sometimes unambitious, and sometimes the ambitious man is praised and sometimes the unambitious. Why this is we will explain afterward; for the present we will follow our plan and enumerate the other types of dispositions.

In feelings of anger we also find excess, deficiency, and moderation. The dispositions themselves hardly have recognized names, but as the moderate man is here called amiable, we will call his disposition amiableness. Of those who go to extremes, we may take the term *wrathful* for the one who is excessive, with wrathfulness for the vice, and *apathetic* for him who is deficient, with apathy for his disposition.

Besides these, there are three kinds of moderation, which bear some resemblance to one another and yet are different. They all have to do with relations in speech and action, but they differ in that

1108a

one has to do with the truthfulness of these relations, while the other two have to do with its pleasantness. One of the two deals with pleasantness in matters of amusement, the other with pleasantness in all the relations of life. We must therefore speak of these qualities also in order that we may more plainly see how, in all cases, moderation is praiseworthy, while the extreme courses are neither right nor praiseworthy, but reprehensible.

In these cases also names are for the most part lacking, but we must try, here as elsewhere, to coin names ourselves, in order to make our argument clear and easy to follow.

In regard to truth, then, let us call him who observes the mean a true or truthful person, and observance of the mean truth or truthfulness. Exaggerating the truth about oneself may be called boasting, and the person a boaster. Understating the truth about oneself may be called self-depreciating and the person a self-depreciator.

An example of "exaggerating the truth about oneself" would be _____ _____ _____.

With regard to pleasantness in amusement, he who observes the mean may be called witty, and his character wittiness. Excess may be called buffoonery, and the man a buffoon; while *humorless* may stand for the person who is deficient, and *humorlessness* for his disposition.

An example of "understating the truth about oneself" would be _____ _____ _____.

With regard to pleasantness in the other affairs of life, he who makes himself properly pleasant may be called friendly, and his moderation friendliness; he that exceeds may be called obsequious if he has no ulterior motive, but a flatterer if he seeks his own advantage. He that is deficient in this respect and always makes himself disagreeable may be called quarrelsome or grouchy.

A mean can also be found in our emotional experiences and our feelings. For example, shame is not a virtue and the modest man is praised. For in these matters also we speak of one man as observing the intermediate, of another man as going beyond it (as the shame-faced man whom the least thing makes shy), while he who is deficient in the feeling of shame, or lacks it altogether, is called shameless, but the term *modest* is applied to him who observes the intermediate.

Righteous indignation, again, strikes the mean between envy and spite. These have to do with feelings of pleasure and pain at what happens to our neighbors. A man is called righteously indignant when he feels pain at the sight of undeserved prosperity, but an envious man goes beyond him and is pained by the sight of anyone in prosperity. The spiteful man is so far from being pained that he actually exults in the misfortunes of his neighbors. We shall have another opportunity to discuss these matters.

1108b

As for *justice*, the term is used in more senses than one. We will, therefore, after disposing of the above questions, distinguish these various senses and show how each of these kinds of justice is a kind of moderation. Then we will treat of the intellectual virtues in the same way.

Complete the following table with ten of Aristotle's examples. Place a dotted line where there is no name for a particular virtue or vice.

	Virtue/Vice	Excess	Mean	Deficiency
1.				
2.				
3.				
4.				
5.				
6.				
7.				
8.				
9.				
10.				

8. What is the relation between the mean and its extremes?

There are, as we said, three classes of dispositions, namely two kinds of vice, one marked by excess, and the other by deficiency, and one kind of virtue, the observance of the mean.

The extreme dispositions are opposed both to the intermediate or moderate disposition and to one another, while the moderate disposition is opposed to both the extremes. Just as a quantity that is equal to a given quantity is also greater when compared with less, and less when compared with a greater quantity, so the intermediate or moderate dispositions exceed as compared with the deficient dispositions and fall short as compared with the excessive dispositions, both in feeling and in action. For example, the courageous man seems foolhardy when compared with the coward and cowardly when compared with the foolhardy. Similarly the self-controlled man appears self-indulgent in comparison with the ascetic and ascetic in comparison with the self-indulgent man. The gener-

Aristotle's point about courage and foolhardiness is _____ _____ _____ .

ous man appears extravagant by the side of the stingy man and stingy by the side of the extravagant man.

So the extreme dispositions try to displace the intermediate or moderate disposition, and each represents the other as falling into the opposite extreme. The coward calls the courageous man foolhardy, the foolhardy calls the other coward, and so on in other cases.

While the intermediate and the extremes are opposed to one another, the extremes are still more opposed to each other than to the mean because they are further removed from one another than from the intermediate....

Sometimes an extreme, when compared with the intermediate, has a sort of resemblance to it, as foolhardiness has to courage or extravagance has to generosity, but there is the greatest possible dissimilarity between the extremes.

Again, "things that are as far as possible removed from each other" is the accepted definition of opposites, so that the further things are removed from each other the more opposite they are.

In comparison with the mean, however, it is sometimes the deficiency that is the more opposed and sometimes the excess. For example, foolhardiness, which is an excess, is not so much opposed to courage as cowardice, which is a deficiency. Indifference, which is lack of feeling, is not so much opposed to self-control as self-indulgence, which is an excess.

1109a

There are two reasons for this. One is the reason derived from the nature of the matter itself: Since one extreme is, in fact, nearer and more similar to the intermediate, we naturally do not oppose it to the intermediate so strongly as the other. For example, as foolhardiness seems more similar to courage and nearer to it, and cowardice more dissimilar, we speak of cowardice as the opposite rather than the other because what is further removed from the intermediate seems to be more opposed to it.

The word "this" refers to _____ _____ _____ .

This, then, is one reason derived from the nature of the thing itself. Another reason lies in ourselves, and it is this: Those things to which we happen to be more prone by nature appear to be more opposed to the mean. For example, our natural inclination is toward indulgence in pleasure, and so we more easily fall into self-indulgence rather than a life of self-control. Those things toward which we have a greater attraction are spoken of as more opposed to the mean. Thus self-indulgence, which is an excess, is more opposed to self-control than the deficiency is.

An example from your life of Aristotle's point in this paragraph is _____ _____ _____ _____ _____ .

Go back over your underlinings and summarize the key ideas in this chapter. Then we will look at some of the key ideas Aristotle has presented so far.

The main points Aristotle made were _____

_____

_____

_____

_____.

Now, state one main point Aristotle has made about each of these topics: (1) ends and means, (2) the chief good, (3) politics, (4) happiness, (5) the function of man, (6) virtue and the vices of excess and deficiency. (Use your notes!)

1. _____

_____.

2. _____

_____.

3. _____

_____.

4. _____

_____.

5. _____

_____.

6. _____

_____.

Like much of the *Nicomachean Ethics,* the next section is full of good, practical advice. Pause after reading each of the nine paragraphs and try to note in the margin how you might apply Aristotle's analysis to your own life.

9. How can the mean be attained?

1._____
_____
_____.

2._____
_____
_____.

We have sufficiently explained, then, that moral virtue is observance of the mean, and in what sense, that is, (1) as holding a middle position between two vices, one on the side of excess and the other on the side of deficiency, and (2) as aiming at the intermediate or moderate amount both in feeling and in action.

Thus it is a hard thing to be good because finding the middle or the intermediate in each case is a hard thing, just as finding the middle or center of a circle is a thing that is not within the power of any but one who has the proper knowledge.

Thus anyone can be angry—that is quite easy—and anyone can give money away or spend it; but to do these things to the right person, in the right amount, at the right time, with the right object, and in the right manner, is not what everybody can do and is by no means easy. That is why right action is rare, praiseworthy, and noble.

He that aims at the intermediate, then, should first of all strive to avoid the extreme that is more opposed to it, as Calypso[17] bids Ulysses,

Clear of that surf and spray keep thy ship.

One extreme is more dangerous and the other less so. Since it is hard to hit the intertmediate precisely, we must "take the next best course," as the proverb has it, and choose the lesser of two evils; that will be best effected in the way we have described.

And also we must consider, each for himself, which errors we are most prone to, for different natures are inclined to different things; this we may learn by the pleasure or pain we feel. Then we must bend ourselves in the opposite direction because by keeping well away from error we shall arrive at the middle course, as we straighten a bent stick by bending it the other way.

In all cases we must be especially on our guard against pleasant things because we cannot be trusted to judge impartially against pleasure. So in our behavior toward pleasure we should imitate the behavior of the old counselors toward Helen,[18] and in all cases repeat their saying, "if we dismiss her we shall make fewer mistakes." This, in outline, is the course by which we shall best be able to hit the intermediate.

But it is a hard task, we must admit, especially in a particular case. It is not easy to determine, for instance, how and with whom one ought to be angry, and upon what grounds, and for how long, because public opinion sometimes praises those who fall short and calls them gentle, and sometimes applies the term *manly* to those who show harsh temper.

In fact a slight error, whether on the side of excess or deficiency, is not blamed, but only a considerable error because then there can be no mistake. But it is hardly possible to determine by reasoning how far or to what extent a man must go wrong to incur blame. Indeed matters that fall within the scope of perception never can be so determined since such matters lie within the region of particulars and can only be determined by perception.

So much then is obvious, that the intermediate state is in all cases to be praised, but that we ought to incline sometimes toward excess,

3. _____
_____
_____.

4. _____
_____
_____.

1109b

5. _____
_____
_____.

6. _____
_____
_____.

7. _____
_____
_____.

8. _____
_____
_____.

9. _____
_____
_____.

sometimes toward deficiency because in this way we shall most easily hit the mean and achieve goodness.

What is the most personally useful thing you can learn from Aristotle in this chapter?

I would have to say _____

_____.

The way I could apply this to my life is _____

_____.

In the next book Aristotle begins an analysis of the voluntary and involuntary aspects of human life. To begin thinking about this, make a list of voluntary and involuntary actions. Then construct a definition of the voluntary and involuntary. Finally, see if you can think of an example of an action that would in some sense be both voluntary and involuntary.

Samples of voluntary actions would be _____

_____

_____.

Examples of involuntary actions would be _____

_____

_____.

Looking at my examples, a good definition of all voluntary action would be _____

_____.

A good definition of involuntary action would be _____

_____

_____.

An action that might have both a voluntary and an involuntary aspect would be _____.

The voluntary part would be _____.

The involuntary part would be _____.

In the following long chapter underline the distinctions Aristotle makes between the voluntary and the involuntary. Early in the chapter he presents an analysis of the voluntary and involuntary components of the same action.

Before going on to Book III, complete this review of chapter questions since the end of Book I.

Book I

13. What are the parts of the soul?

_____

_____

_____ .

Book II

1. How is moral virtue acquired?

_____

_____ .

2. Your title:_____

_____

_____ .

4. How does one become virtuous?

_____

_____ .

5. What genus or class does virtue belong to?

_____

_____ .

6. How can virtue be more precisely defined?

_____

_____ .

7. What are some examples of virtues and vices?

_____

_____ .

8. What is the relation between the mean and its extremes?

_____

_____ .

9. How can the mean be attained?

_____

_____ .

Book III
Moral Responsibility

1A. What are the characteristics of voluntary and involuntary actions?

Virtue, as we have seen, has to do with feelings and actions. Now praise or blame is given only to what is voluntary; whatever is involuntary receives pardon and sometimes even pity.

It seems, therefore, that a clear distinction between the voluntary and the involuntary is necessary for those who are investigating the nature of virtue, and will also help legislators in assigning rewards and punishments.

The involuntary is generally held to be what is done under compulsion or through ignorance.

"Done under compulsion" means that the cause is external, the individual or person contributing nothing toward it; as, for instance, if he were carried somewhere by a whirlwind or by men whom he could not resist.

But there is some question about acts done to avoid a greater evil or to obtain some noble end. For example, if a tyrant were to order you to do something disgraceful, having your parents or children in his power—who were to live if you did it, but to die if you did not—it is a matter of dispute whether such acts are involuntary or voluntary. Throwing a cargo overboard in a storm is a somewhat similar case. No one voluntarily throws away his property if nothing is to come of it, but any sensible person would do so to save the life of himself and the crew.

Acts of this kind, then, are of a mixed nature, but they more nearly resemble voluntary acts. They are desired or chosen at the time they are done, and the end or motive of an act is that which is

1110a

An example of an involuntary action would be _____
_____
_____.
An example of a voluntary action would be _____
_____
_____
_____.

the end at the moment of performing the act. In applying the terms *voluntary* and *involuntary*, therefore, we must consider the state of the individual's mind at the time....{In the acts we just described, the individual} wills the act at the time because the cause that sets the limbs going lies in the individual in such cases, and where the cause lies in the individual, it rests with him to do or not to do.

Such acts, then, are voluntary, though in themselves (or apart from these qualifying circumstances) we may allow them to be involuntary because no one would choose anything of this kind on its own account.

In fact for actions of this sort men are sometimes praised—for example, when they endure something disgraceful or painful in order to secure some great and noble result—but in the opposite case they are blamed, because no worthy person would endure extreme disgrace when there was no noble result in view, or only a trifling one.

The words "this sort" refer to

_____

_____

_____.

But in some cases we do not praise but pardon—for example, when a man is induced to do a wrong act by pressure that is too strong for human nature and that no one could bear. Nonetheless, there are some cases of this kind, I think, where the plea of compulsion is inadmissible, and where, rather than do the act, a man should suffer death in its most painful form. For example, the circumstances that "compelled" Alcmaeon in Euripides[19] to kill his mother seem absurd.

Pause here for a moment.

What was Aristotle's initial definition of involuntary actions?

He says, "_____

_____."

Assume you are in the position he describes. A tyrant holds your parents and orders you to do something disgraceful, kill a friend, for example. If you do not your parents will die. If you killed the friend, in what sense would your action be voluntary, and in what sense would it be involuntary? And what does Aristotle decide about cases of this kind?

Killing my friend would be voluntary in the sense that _____

_____.

It would be involuntary in the sense that _____

_____.

Aristotle's view is that _____

_____.

Now read his analysis of compulsory acts.

1B. What is the nature of compulsory acts?

It is sometimes hard to decide whether we should do this deed to avoid this evil, or whether we should endure this evil rather than do this deed; but it is still harder to abide by our decisions. Generally the evil that we wish to avoid is something painful, the deed we are pressed to do is something disgraceful. Hence we are blamed or praised based on whether we do or do not succumb to the compulsion.

What kinds of acts, then, are to be called compulsory?

1110b

Underline key points about compulsory acts.

I think our answer must be that, in the first place—when the cause lies outside and the individual has no part in it—the act is called compulsory without qualification (and therefore involuntary); but that, in the second place—when an act that would not be voluntarily done for its own sake is chosen now in preference to a given alternative, the cause lying in the individual—such an act should be described as involuntary in itself, or in the abstract involuntary but now, and in preference to this alternative, voluntary. An act of the latter kind is more like the nature of a voluntary act, for acts fall within the sphere of particulars and here the particular thing that is done is voluntary.

It is scarcely possible, however, to lay down rules for determining which of two alternatives is to be preferred, because there are many differences in particular cases.

It might be suggested that acts whose motive is something pleasant or noble are compulsory, for here we are controlled by something outside us. But if this were so, all our acts would be compulsory because these are the motives of every act of every man.

Why would "all our acts" be compulsory? _____
_____
_____
_____.

Again, acting under compulsion and against one's will is painful, but action whose motive is something pleasant or noble involves pleasure.

It is absurd, therefore, to blame things outside us instead of our own readiness to yield to their allurements, and, while we claim our noble acts as our own, to set down our disgraceful actions to "pleasant things outside us."

Compulsory actions, then, are actions in which the person contributes nothing and the cause is external.

In this last paragraph Aristotle defined compulsory actions. Create three of your own examples and then contrast these to voluntary actions.

Three compulsory actions would be _____
_____
_____.

Three voluntary actions would be _____

_____

_____.

The essential difference between the former and the latter is not just that the former are compulsory and the latter are voluntary,

but also that all the former share the characteristic of _____

_____ and all the latter

share the characteristic of _____.

In the section you just read, Aristotle raises the interesting argument that "it might be suggested that acts whose motive is something pleasant or noble are compulsory, for here we are controlled by something outside us. But if this were so, all our acts would be compulsory because these are the motives of every act of every man."

State this argument in your own words and offer an example of an action to which it might apply. Then reread the arguments Aristotle offers against this view and state one of these in your own words.

In the section you just quoted Aristotle is presenting a view he

doesn't agree with. The view is _____

_____

_____.

After rereading his arguments against this position, I think

one of these arguments could be restated as _____

_____

_____.

Now carefully read the final section of this chapter. When you finish, decide what the major subject was and write a title below in the form of a question.

1C.

What is done through ignorance is always "nonvoluntary," but is involuntary" when the individual is pained afterward and sorry when he finds what he has done. For when a man who has done something through ignorance is not ashamed about what he has done you cannot say that he did it voluntarily, since he did not know what he was doing, but neither can you say that he did it involuntarily or unwillingly, since he is not sorry.

The difference between "nonvoluntary" and "involuntary" is _____
_____
_____
_____.

Another example of the difference between acting through ignorance and acting in ignorance would be

_____

_____

_____

and _____

_____

_____

_____ .

1111a

All of Aristotle's examples in this

paragraph are examples of _____

_____

_____ .

If a man who has acted through ignorance, then, is sorry afterward, he is held to have done the deed involuntarily or unwillingly; if he is not sorry afterward, we may say, to mark the distinction, that he did the deed "nonvoluntarily"; for, as the case is different, it is better to have a distinct name.

Acting *through* ignorance, however, seems to be different from acting *in* ignorance. For instance, when a man is drunk or in a rage he is not thought to act *through* ignorance, but through intoxication or rage, and yet not knowingly, but *in* ignorance.

Indeed every wicked man is ignorant of what should be done, and it is this kind of error that makes men unjust and bad generally. But the term *involuntary* is not properly applied to cases in which a man is ignorant of what is for his own good. The ignorance that makes an act involuntary is not this general ignorance of the principles that should determine preference (this constitutes vice)—not, I say, this ignorance of the universal (for we blame a man for this)—but ignorance of the particular occasion and circumstances of the action. These are the grounds of pity and pardon, because he who is ignorant of any of these particulars acts involuntarily.

Next we should specify what these particulars are and how many. They are (1) the doer; (2) the deed; and (3) the circumstance or occasion of it; sometimes they also include the instrument (for example, the tool) with which it is done, that for the sake of which it is done (for example, for protection), and the way in which it is done (for example, gently or violently).

Now, a man cannot (unless he is mad) be ignorant of all these particulars; for example, he evidently cannot be ignorant of the doer because he must know himself.

But a man may be ignorant of what he is doing. For example, a man who has said something will sometimes plead that the words slipped out of his mouth or that he did not know that the subject was forbidden, as Aeschylus pleaded in the case of the Mysteries. Or a man might plead that when he discharged the weapon he only intended to show how it worked, as the prisoner did in the catapult case. Again a man might mistake his son for an enemy, as Merope did, or a sharp spear for one with a blunted point, or a heavy stone for a pumice stone. Again, someone might kill a man with a blow intended to save him or strike a serious blow when wishing only to show how a blow would be delivered, as boxers do when they spar with open hands.

Ignorance, then, being possible with regard to all these circumstances, he who is ignorant of any of them is held to have acted involuntarily, and especially when he is ignorant of the most important particulars, which are generally taken to be the act and the effect of the act.

Besides this, however, the individual must be sorry and regretful for what he has done, if the ignorantly committed act is to be called involuntary (not merely nonvoluntary).

But now, having found that an act is involuntary when done under compulsion or through ignorance, we may conclude that a voluntary act is one that is initiated by the doer with knowledge of the particular circumstances of the act. I believe that it is incorrect to say that acts done through anger or desire are involuntary.

In the first place, if this be true, we can no longer agree that any of the other animals, or even children, act voluntarily.

Again, does this view mean that none of the acts that we do through desire or anger are voluntary, or that the noble ones are voluntary and the disgraceful ones involuntary? Interpreted in the latter sense, it is surely ridiculous, as one man is the author of both. If we take the former interpretation, it is absurd, I think, to say that we should desire a thing, and also to say that its pursuit is involuntary; but, in fact, there are things at which we should be angry, and things that we should desire such as health and learning.

Again, it seems that what is done unwillingly is painful, while what is done through desire is pleasant.

Again, what difference is there, in the case of involuntariness, between wrong deeds done through calculation and wrong deeds done in anger? Both are to be avoided, and our unreasoning passions or feelings seem to be just as much our own as our reasonings or calculations.

But the fact is that all human actions proceed either from passion or from appetite: To make all such actions involuntary would be too absurd.

The "former interpretation" is _____
_____
_____ .

1111b

In this section Aristotle defines involuntary actions as those "done under compulsion or through ignorance." We have already considered actions done under compulsion. What are some examples of actions done *through* ignorance and how does he distinguish these actions from those done *in* ignorance?

Some of his examples of acts done through ignorance are

_____
_____ .

Two of my own would be _____
_____ .

The difference between these actions done *through* ignorance and an action like _____ done *in* ignorance is _____

_____.

> Before going on to the next section try again to solve a problem Aristotle confronts. He is about to distinguish between acting from choice and acting from desire, anger, wish, and opinion. Try to distinguish between acting from choice and acting from desire.
>
> An example of an action from choice is when I choose to
>
> _____.
>
> An example of an action driven by desire would be _____
>
> _____.
>
> The essential difference between the two would be _____
>
> _____. Incidentally, both
>
> of these are different from acting from wish because _____
>
> _____.

2A. What is the difference between acting from choice and acting from desire, anger, wish, or opinion?

1111b4

Number each of Aristotle's key points in this chapter.

Now that we have distinguished voluntary from involuntary acts, our next task is to discuss choice, because it seems to be most intimately connected with virtue and to be a surer test of character than action itself.

It seems that *choosing* is *willing*, but that the two terms are not identical, *willing* being the wider. Children and other animals have will but not choice; and acts done on the spur of the moment are said to be voluntary but not to be done with deliberate choice.

Those who say that choice is desire, anger, wish, or an opinion of some sort do not seem to give a correct account of it.

In the first place, choice is not shared by irrational creatures, but desire and passion are.

Again, the morally weak man acts from desire and not from choice; the morally strong man acts from choice and not from desire.

Again, desire may be opposite to choice, but one desire cannot be opposite to another desire.[20]

Again, the object of desire (or aversion) is the pleasant or the painful, but the object of choice (as such) is neither painful nor pleasant.

Still less can choice be anger because acts done in anger seem to be least of all done from deliberate choice.

Nor is choice wish, though it seems very similar because we cannot deliberately choose the impossible, and a man who said that he did would be thought a fool; but we may wish for the impossible, for example, to escape death.

Again, while we may wish what never could be produced by our own efforts (for example, the success of a particular actor or athlete), we never deliberately choose such things but only those that we think may be produced by our own efforts.

Again, we are said to wish the end but to choose the means. For example, we wish to be healthy, but we choose what will make us healthy. We wish to be happy…but it would not be correct to say we deliberately choose to be happy because we say that choice deals with what is in our power.

The difference between choice and wish is that choice is _____
_____
_____
_____
while wish is _____
_____
_____
_____.

In this section Aristotle tries to show that choice is different from desire, anger, and wish. Select one argument that distinguishes each from choice.

According to Aristotle choice cannot be desire because _____

_____.

Choice cannot be anger because _____

_____.

Choice cannot be wish because _____

_____.

One of Aristotle's strengths is his ability to come up with a remarkable variety of supporting arguments. In the next section he offers seven reasons why choice is not the same thing as opinion. An example of each may help you understand the points he is making. I choose to go to school; it is my opinion that going to school is good. These two are clearly different but it not easy to say exactly why.

One difference is _____

_____.

In the next section pause after each of Aristotle's distinctions between choice and opinion and put them in your own words.

2B. What are the differences between choice and opinion?

Nor can choice be opinion because, in the first place, anything may be a matter of opinion—what is unalterable and impossible no less than what is in our power—and, in the second place, we distinguish

An example of a choice would be

_____

_____.

An example of an opinion would be

_____

_____.

opinions based on whether they are true or false, not on whether they are good or bad, as we do with choice.

His first two distinctions are?

First he says _____

_____.

Secondly he says _____

_____.

We may say, then, that choice is not the same as opinion in general; nor, indeed, does anyone maintain this.

But, further, it is not identical with a particular kind of opinion. For our choice of good or evil makes us morally good or bad; holding certain opinions does not.

Here he is saying _____

_____.

Again, we choose to take or to avoid a good or bad object, and so on; but we form opinions about what its nature is, or what it is useful for, or in what way it is useful; but we cannot form opinions to take or to avoid it.

His point is _____

_____.

Again, a choice is praised for its rightness or correctness, an opinion for its truth.

An example of his point here would be _____

_____.

Again, we choose a thing when we know well that it is good; we may have an opinion about a thing of which we know nothing.

For example, _____.

Thus, his point is _____

_____.

Again, it seems that those who are best at choosing are not always the best at forming opinions, but that some who hold correct opinions fail, through moral depravity, to choose what they should.

To illustrate this argument let us say I _____

_____.

Aristotle's point would be _____

_____.

It may be said that choice must be preceded or accompanied by an opinion or judgment; but this makes no difference: Our question is not that, but whether they are identical.

What, then, is choice, since it is none of these?

It seems, as we said, that what is chosen is willed but that what is willed is not always deliberately chosen.

May we define choice as {an action that is} the result of previous deliberation? {It seems so} for a choice implies calculation and reasoning. The name itself, too, seems to indicate this, implying that something is chosen before or in preference to other things.

Thus, what is the essential characteristic of acting from choice?

Looking at Aristotle's last few sentences I would have to say

it is _____.

Aristotle considers deliberation in the next section. Obviously we can deliberate about the best way to get a good grade on a test but we cannot deliberate about whether the teacher will give the test. Think of a few other examples of things we can and cannot deliberate about.

I can deliberate about _____.

But I cannot deliberate about _____.

I could also deliberate about _____,

but I obviously could not deliberate about _____.

See if you solve this problem in the same way as Aristotle. Let us say you were a doctor. As a doctor would you deliberate about the ends of the practice of medicine or about the means?

Good question. I would say _____

because _____.

Now see what Aristotle says.

3. What are the differences between things we can and cannot deliberate about?

Now, as to deliberation, do we deliberate about everything, and may anything whatever be subject for deliberation, or are there some things about which deliberation is impossible?

By "subject for deliberation" we should understand, I think, not what a fool or a maniac, but what a rational being would deliberate about.

Now nobody deliberates about eternal or unalterable things, for example, the system of the heavenly bodies, or the incommensurability of the side and the diagonal of a square.

Again, no one deliberates about things that change if they always change in the same way (whether the cause of change be necessity, nature, or any other cause), for example, the solstices and the sunrise; or about things that are quite irregular, like drought and rain; or about matters of chance, like the finding of a treasure.

Again, even human affairs are not always a matter of deliberation. For example, what would be the best constitution for Scythia is a question that no Spartan would deliberate about.

The reason we do not deliberate about these things is that none of them are things that we can ourselves control.

But things that we do deliberate about are things that are within our power and that can be realized by our actions. And these are the only things that remain because besides nature, necessity, and chance, the only remaining cause of change is reason and human action in general....

A further limitation is that where there is exact and absolute knowledge, there is no room for deliberation. For example, spelling, for there is no doubt how the letters should be put together.

We deliberate, then, about things that are brought about by our own efforts, but not always in the same way. For example, {we deliberate} about medicine and money-making, and about navigation more than about physical training, because navigation has not yet been reduced to an exact set of principles, and so on; but {we deliberate} more about matters of art than matters of science, as there is more doubt about them.

Matters of deliberation, then, are matters in which there are rules that generally hold good, but in which the result cannot be predicted, that is, in which there is an element of uncertainty. In important matters we call in advisers, distrusting our own powers of judgment.

It is not about ends, but about means that we deliberate. A physician does not deliberate whether he shall heal, or an orator whether he shall persuade, or a statesman whether he shall make a good system of laws, or a man in any other profession about his end. But

The kinds of subjects we don't deliberate about are _____

_____

_____

_____

because _____

_____

_____ .

1112b

The kinds of subjects we do deliberate about are _____

_____

_____

_____

because _____

_____

_____

_____ .

having some particular end in view, we consider how and by what means this end can be attained. If it appears that it can be attained by various means, we further consider which is the easiest and best; but if it can only be attained by one means, we consider how it is to be attained by this means, and how this means itself is to be guaranteed, and so on, until we come to the first in the chain of causes, although it is last in the order of discovery.

In deliberation we seem to inquire and to analyze in the way described, just as we analyze a geometrical figure to learn how to construct it. And though investigation is not always deliberation—mathematical investigation, for instance, is not—deliberation is always investigation; what is last in the analysis coming first in the order of construction....

Now it appears that a man, as we have already said, is the source of his acts; that he deliberates about what he can do himself, and that what he does is done for the sake of something else. From this it follows that he does not deliberate about the end, but about the means to the end.

Again, he does not deliberate about particular facts, for example, whether this be a loaf of bread, or whether it it has been long enough in the oven. These are matters of immediate perception, and if he goes on deliberating forever he will never come to a conclusion....

Since, then, a thing is said to be chosen when, being in our power, it is desired after deliberation, choice may be defined as deliberate desire for something within our power, because we first deliberate, and then, having made our decision thereupon, we desire the object we have deliberated about.

Let this stand, then, for an account in outline of choice and of the ends and means it deals with.

An example of deliberating about the means and not the end would be

_____

_____.

1113a

Aristotle says, "For we cannot deliberate about ends but about the means by which ends can be attained."

Aristotle means _____

_____. For example,

here is an end: _____. The means to

this end would be: _____.

I can deliberate about the means because _____

_____. I cannot deliberate about

the end because _____

_____. The way he would apply this

to the practice of medicine is _____.

In the next short section Aristotle expands one of the key ideas in the *Nicomachean Ethics*: the judgments of the man of good character as the standard of ethical choices. He begins by distinguishing between our wish for something that *is* good and our wish for something that is only *apparently* good. If you are an alcoholic and you wish for a drink, you wish for something that you think is good when in fact it is only apparently good. If you are an individual of good character and you wish to spend your life in the study of philosophy, then, according to Aristotle, you wish for a real and genuine good. This seems simple enough but it leads to two problems, which Aristotle proceeds to solve. One problem has to do with those who hold that an individual always wishes for what is absolutely good and not for what is apparently good. The other problem has to do with those who hold that an individual can wish only for what seems good (the apparently good) and that there is no way of determining what is absolutely good.

4. In what sense is the object of wish the good, and in what sense is it the apparent good?

Wish, we have already said, is for the end, but whereas some hold that the object of wish is the good, others hold that it is what seems good.

Those who maintain that the object of wish is the good have to admit that what those wish for who choose wrongly is not the object of wish (for if so it would be good; but it may so happen that it was bad); on the other hand, those who maintain that the object of wish is what seems good have to admit that there is nothing that is naturally the {best} object of wish, but that each wishes for what seems good to him—different and even opposite things seeming good to different people.

As neither of these alternatives quite satisfies us, perhaps we had better say that the good is the real {and best} object of wish (without any qualifying phrase), but that what seems good is the object of wish to each man. The man of good character, then, wishes for the real {and best} object of wish; but what the bad man wishes for may be anything whatever, just as, with regard to the body, those who are in good condition find those things healthy that are really healthy, while those who are diseased find other things healthy (and it is the same with things bitter, sweet, hot, heavy, etc.). For the man of good character judges each case correctly, and in each case what is actually true is also what appears true to him.

Corresponding to each of our dispositions there is a special form of the noble and the pleasant, and perhaps there is nothing so

The similarity between a person of good character and a person in good condition is _____

_____

_____

_____ .

distinctive of the man of good character as the power he has of discerning these special forms in each case, being himself, as it were, their standard and measure.

In most cases what misleads people seems to be pleasure; it seems to be a good thing, even when it is not. So they choose what is pleasant as good and shun pain as evil. 1113b

This will be one of the hardest tasks in the *Nicomachean Ethics*. Take some time, slowly reread Chapter 4, and then for each of the five paragraphs state exactly what Aristotle is saying.

The first paragraph is not very difficult. The point Aristotle is

making is _____

_____.

The second paragraph is more challenging. In general what he is

talking about is _____

_____. Specifically, what he seems to be

saying is _____

_____

_____.

His main points in each of the other paragraphs are: _____

_____

_____

_____

_____

_____

_____

_____.

5. What is the nature of voluntary actions and our responsibility?

We have seen that while we wish for the end, we deliberate on and choose the means.

Actions that are concerned with means, then, will be guided by choice, and so will be voluntary.

But the acts in which the virtues are manifested are concerned with means.[21] Therefore virtue and vice depend on ourselves. For where it is in our power to act, it is in our power not to act. Where we can say no, we can say yes. If then the doing of a deed, which is noble, is in our power, the not doing of it, which is disgraceful, is also in our power; and if the not doing, which is noble, is in our power, the doing, which is disgraceful, is also in our power. But if the doing and likewise the not doing of noble or base deeds is in our power, and if this is, as we found, identical with being good or bad, then it follows that it is in our power to be worthy or worthless men.

And so the saying—

None would be wicked, none would not be blessed.

seems partly false and partly true: No one indeed is blessed against his will; but vice is voluntary.

If we deny this, we must dispute the statements made just now and must contend that man is not the originator and the parent of his actions as he is parent of his children.

An individual is to actions as a parent is to children because both

_____
_____
_____
_____ .

But if those statements recommend themselves to us, and if we are unable to trace our acts to any other sources than those that depend on ourselves, then actions whose source is within us must depend on us and be voluntary.

This seems to be attested to, moreover, by each one of us in private life, and also by the legislators because they correct and punish those that do evil (except when it is done under compulsion, or through ignorance for which the individual is not responsible) and honor those that do noble deeds, evidently intending to encourage the one sort and discourage the other. But no one encourages us to do that which does not depend on ourselves and is not voluntary. It would be useless to be persuaded not to feel heat, pain, hunger, and so on, as we should feel them all the same.

I say "ignorance for which the individual is *not* responsible" {above in parentheses}, for the ignorance itself is punished by the law if the individual appears to be responsible for his ignorance. For example, the penalty is doubled for an offense committed in a fit of drunkenness because the origin of the offense lies in the man himself. The reason is that he might have avoided the intoxication that was the cause of his ignorance. Again, ignorance of the law, which a man should know and easily can know, does not permit him to escape punishment. It is the same in other cases; where ignorance seems to be the result of negligence, the offender is punished because it was his responsibility to remove this ignorance and he should have taken the necessary trouble.

It may be objected that it was the man's character not to take the trouble {and thus he is not responsible because he has no control over his character}.

We reply that men are themselves responsible for acquiring such a character by their immoral lifestyle, and for being unjust or

1114a

self-indulgent because of repeated acts of wrong or of spending their time in drinking and so on, because it is repeated acts of a particular kind that give a man a particular character.

This is shown by the way in which men train themselves for any kind of contest or performance: They practice continually.

Not to know, then, that repeated acts of this or that kind produce a corresponding character or habit, shows a complete lack of sense.

Moreover, it is absurd to say that he who acts unjustly does not wish to be unjust, or that he who behaves self-indulgently does not wish to be self-indulgent.

{1} If a man knowingly does acts that must make him unjust, he will be voluntarily unjust, but it does not follow that, if he wishes it, he can cease to be unjust and become just, any more than he who is sick can, if he wishes it, be healthy. It may be that he is voluntarily sick through living a dissolute life and disobeying the doctor. At one time, then, he had the option not to be sick, but he no longer has it now that he has thrown away his health. When you have discharged a stone it is no longer in your power to call it back, but nevertheless the throwing and casting away of that stone rest with you because the beginning of its flight depended on you.

In the same way the unjust or the self-indulgent man at the beginning was free not to acquire this character, and therefore he is voluntarily unjust or self-indulgent. But now that he has acquired {this character}, he is no longer free to escape it.

It is not only our moral vices that are voluntary. Bodily vices are also sometimes voluntary and then are subject to blame. We do not blame natural ugliness, but we do blame ugliness that is due to negligence and lack of exercise. It is the same with weakness and infirmity. We should never blame a man who was born blind or lost his sight in an illness or by a blow—we should rather pity him—but we should all blame a man who had blinded himself by excessive drinking or any other kind of self-indulgence.

We see, then, that of the vices of the body it is those that depend on ourselves that are blamed, while those that do not depend on ourselves are not blamed. And if this be so, then in other fields also those vices that are blamed must depend on ourselves.

Some people may perhaps object to this.

{2} "All men," they say, "desire that which appears good to them, but cannot control this appearance; a man's character, whatever it is, decides what shall appear to him to be the good."

I answer, if each man is in some way responsible for his habits or character, then in some way he must be responsible for what appears good to him.

But if this is not the case, then a man is not responsible for, or is not the cause of, his own evil doing; it is through ignorance of the end that he does evil, believing that thereby he will secure the

The main points he is making in {1} are: _____

_____

_____

_____

_____

_____

_____

_____

_____

_____ .

The argument in {2} is: _____

_____

_____

1114b _____

_____

_____

_____ .

greatest good. The striving toward the true end does not depend on our own choice, but a man must be born with a gift of moral vision, so to speak, if he is to discriminate rightly and to choose what is really good. He is truly wellborn who is by nature richly endowed with this gift. It is the greatest and the fairest gift, which we cannot acquire or learn from another, but must keep all our lives just as nature gave it to us, to be well and nobly born in this respect is to be wellborn in the truest and completest sense.

The words "this gift" refer to _____ _____ _____.

Now, granting this to be true, how will virtue be any more voluntary than vice?

For whether it is nature or anything else that determines what shall appear to be the end, it is determined in the same way for both alike, for the good man as for the bad, and both alike refer all their acts of whatever kind to it.

And so whether we hold that it is not merely nature that decides what appears to each to be the end (whatever that be), but that the man himself contributes something; or whether we hold that the end is fixed by nature, but that virtue is voluntary, inasmuch as the good man voluntarily takes the steps to the end—in either case vice will be just as voluntary as virtue. The bad man just as much as the good man is free in choosing particular acts, if not in choosing his own particular end.

An example of virtuous actions creating an individual's character

would be _____ _____ _____ _____ _____.

The way this character might

determine its "end" would be _____ _____ _____ _____ _____ _____ _____.

1115a

If then, as is generally believed, the virtues are voluntary because we do in some way help make our character and being of a certain character determines our idea of the end, the vices also must be voluntary because all this applies equally to them.

We have thus described in outline the nature of the virtues in general. They are forms of moderation or modes of observing the mean, and they are dispositions. We have shown what produces them, how they themselves result in the performance of the same acts that produce them, that they depend on ourselves and are voluntary, and that they follow the guidance of right reason.

But our actions are not voluntary in the same sense as our dispositions.

We are masters of our acts from beginning to end when we know the particular circumstances, but we are masters of only the beginning of our dispositions, while their growth by gradual steps is imperceptible, like the growth of disease. Inasmuch, however, as it was in our power to use or not to use our faculties in this way, the resulting dispositions are therefore voluntary.

Let's look carefully at two sections of this long and important chapter. At the paragraph that starts at {1} Aristotle makes a triple comparison. He compares a man who disobeys a doctor's orders to one who throws a stone, and to an unjust man. What point is he making?

There is a point at which a sick man could make himself well by following a doctor's orders and a point at which he can no longer control the effects of his illness. Similarly, in the case of

throwing a stone _____

_____ .

Similarly, in the case of an unjust man _____

_____ .

The general point Aristotle is making in all three of these cases is

_____ .

The specific point he is making about voluntary and involuntary

actions in the case of an unjust man is _____

_____ .

Interesting. Now look equally closely at the section that begins with {2} Aristotle offers a counterargument to the view he has been presenting that an individual is responsible for his or her choices. {Note: because of the status of women in the ancient world, when Aristotle says "men" he does not mean "men and women."} The counterargument is that when we desire something (let us say we are alcoholics and we desire a drink), we desire what appears to us to be the good. But it is our character, our personality, that determines what appears to be the good; therefore when we choose to take a drink, we are not responsible because our actions are controlled by our personality and we have no control over our personality. The obvious conclusion is that we cannot be blamed for any of our bad actions because all we have done is choose what we thought was good, and our personality, our way of seeing the world, created this false impression.

Return to {2} and read Aristotle's refutation of this argument. How does he do it?

The strongest argument Aristotle makes against this view is

_____

_____ .

An example of what he means would be _____

_____ .

Therefore, _____

_____

_____ .

The next three short chapters are about courage. At each asterisk in the column, put Aristotle's point into your own words.

6. What are the characteristics of courage?

Now let us take up each of the virtues again in turn and say what it is, what its subject is, and how it deals with it. In doing this, we shall at the same time see how many they are.

First of all let us take courage.

We have already said that it is moderation or observance of the mean with regard to feelings of fear and confidence.

Now, fear evidently is aroused by fearful things, and these are, roughly speaking, evil things; so fear is sometimes defined as "anticipation of evil."

Fear, then, is aroused by evil of any kind—for example, by disgrace, poverty, disease, friendlessness, and death—but it does not appear that every kind of evil gives an opportunity for courage. There are things that we actually should fear, that it is noble to fear and base not to fear—for example, disgrace. He who fears disgrace is an honorable man with a proper sense of shame, while he who does not fear it is shameless (though some people stretch the word *courageous* so far as to apply it to him because he has a certain resemblance to the courageous man, courage also being a kind of fearlessness). Poverty, perhaps, we should not fear, nor disease, nor generally those things that are not the result of vice and do not depend on ourselves. But to be fearless in regard to these things is not strictly courage, though here also the term is sometimes applied because of a certain resemblance. There are people, for example, who, though cowardly in the presence of the dangers of war, are generous and face the loss of money bravely.

On the other hand, a man is not to be called cowardly for fearing brutality to his children or his wife, or the effects of others' envy toward himself and things of that kind, nor virtuously courageous for being unmoved when he is about to be flogged.

In what kind of terrors, then, does the courageous man display his virtue? Surely in the greatest because no one is more able to endure what is terrible. Of all things the most terrible is death, because death is the end, and when a man is dead it seems that there is no longer either good or evil for him.

It seems, however, that even death does not on all occasions give opportunity for courage, for example, death by water or by disease.

On what occasions then? Surely on the noblest occasions, and those are the occasions that occur in war because they involve the greatest and the noblest danger.

This is confirmed by the honors that courage receives in free states and at the hands of rulers.

The term *courageous*, then, in the strict sense, will be applied to him who fearlessly faces an honorable death and all emergencies that might involve sudden death, and such emergencies mostly occur in war.

Of course, the courageous man is also fearless in the presence of illness and at sea, but in a different way from sailors. Because of their experience sailors are full of hope when landsmen are already despairing for their lives and filled with revulsion at the thought of such a death.

1115b

Moreover, the circumstances that especially call out courage are those in which one can put up a fight or in which death is noble; but in the case of death by drowning or illness there is neither nobility nor room for a soldier's prowess.

* _____
_____
_____
_____.

7. What are additional characteristics of courage and also of its opposite?

Fear is not aroused in all men by the same things, yet we commonly speak of fearful things that surpass human endurance. Such things, then, inspire fear in every rational man. But the fearful things that a man may face differ in importance and also in being more or less fearful, and so it is with the things that inspire confidence. Now the courageous man always keeps his presence of mind as far as a man can. So though he will fear these fearful things, he will endure them as he should and as reason bids him, for the sake of the noble because this is the end or goal of virtue.

But it is possible to fear these things too much or too little and also to take as fearful what is not really so. Thus men fall into error sometimes by fearing the wrong things, sometimes by fearing in the wrong manner or at the wrong time, and so on. All this applies equally to things that inspire confidence.

* _____
_____
_____
_____
_____.

He, then, who endures and fears what he should from the right motive, in the right manner, and at the right time, and feels confidence in the same ways, is courageous. The courageous man regulates both his feeling and his action according to the nature of each case as reason bids him….

To the courageous man courage is essentially a fair or noble thing. Therefore the end or motive of his courage is also noble because everything takes its character from its end.

It is from a noble motive, therefore, that the courageous man endures and acts courageously in each particular case.

Of the dispositions that run to excess, he that exceeds in fearlessness has no name and this is often the case, as we have said before; but a man would be either a maniac or quite insensible to pain who should fear nothing, not even earthquakes and wild seas, as they say is the case with the Celts.

An example of someone who "exceeds in fearlessness" would be someone who _____ _____.

He who is overconfident in the presence of fearful things is called foolhardy. But the foolhardy man is generally thought to be really a braggart and to pretend to have courage when he does not. He wishes to seem what the courageous man really is in the presence of danger, therefore he imitates him where he can. A foolhardy man is generally a coward at bottom: He swaggers or blusters as long as he can do so safely, but turns tail when real danger comes.

He who is overfearful is a coward because he fears the wrong things, and in the wrong way, etc.

He is also deficient in confidence, but his disposition most clearly displays itself in excess of fear in the presence of pain.

The coward is also pessimistic because he is frightened at everything. But it is the opposite with the courageous man because confidence implies optimism.

Thus the coward and the foolhardy and the courageous man display their characters in the same circumstances, {though} behaving differently under them. While the first two exceed or fall short, the last behaves moderately and as he should; and while the foolhardy are impetuous and eager before danger comes but run away in its presence, the courageous are gallant in action but quiet beforehand.

Courage, then, as we have said, is observance of the mean with regard to things that arouse confidence or fear, under the circumstances that we have specified. The courageous man chooses his course and sticks to his duty because it is noble to do so, or because it is disgraceful not to do so.

But to seek death as a refuge from poverty, love, or any painful thing, is not the act of a brave man, but of a coward. It is unmanly softness to fly from troubles. In such a case death is accepted not because it is noble, but simply as an escape from evil.

9. What is the relationship between courage and pleasure and pain?

Courage is concerned, as we said, with feelings both of confidence and of fear, yet it is not equally concerned with both but more with occasions of fear. It is the man who is calm and behaves as he should on such occasions who is called courageous, rather than he who behaves in this way on occasions that inspire confidence.

And so, as we said, men are called courageous for enduring painful things. Courage, therefore, brings pain and is justly praised because it is harder to endure what is painful than to abstain from what is pleasant.

I do not, of course, mean to say that the end of courage is not pleasant but that it seems to be hidden from view by the attendant circumstances, as is the case in gymnastic contests. Boxers, for

margin notes:

1116a

*
_____
_____
_____.

Aristotle would not say cowardliness was "the observance of the mean" because _____
_____
_____
_____.

1116a14

1117a28

1117b

instance, have a pleasant end in view for which they strive—the crown of victory and the honors—but the blows they receive are painful since the boxers are made of flesh and blood, and so are all the labors they undergo; and as the latter are many, the end appears small, and the pleasantness of the end is hardly apparent.

If, then, the case of courage is similar, death and wounds will be painful to the courageous man and against his will, but he endures them because it is noble to do so or base not to do so.

And the more he is endowed with every virtue, and the happier he is, the more painful death will be to him because life is more worth living to a man of his sort than to anyone else. He deprives himself knowingly of the very best things, and it is painful to do that. But he is not less courageous because he feels this pain; no, we may say he is even more courageous, because in spite of it he chooses noble conduct in battle in preference to those good things.

Thus we see that the rule that the exercise of a virtue is pleasant does not apply to all the virtues, except insofar as the end is attained.

Still, perhaps men of this character may be less efficient as soldiers than those who are not so courageous but have nothing good to lose, because such men are reckless of risk and will sell their lives for a small price.

Here let us close our account of courage. It will not be hard to gather an outline of its nature from what we have said.

The words "this character" refer to

_____

_____

_____.

Look back at your notes for each of the last three chapters and select a few major points.

The main points Aristotle makes about courage in Chapter 6

are _____

_____

_____.

The main points he makes in Chapter 7 are _____

_____

_____

_____.

The main points Aristotle makes in Chapter 9 are _____

_____

_____

_____.

In the next two chapters, Aristotle discusses a new virtue, which in Greek is *sophrosyne*. This is a key word both for Aristotle and for Greek culture. It means literally, "soundness of mind," but because this conveys no particular quality very clearly, *sophrosyne* is also translated as *self-control, temperance,* or even *self-mastery. Self-knowing* might also be used in some places. The problem with using the terms *self-control* and *temperance* to translate *sophrosyne* is that they conjure up an image that is not fully positive and may even seem a bit inhibited to us. Someone who is self-controlled and temperate sounds straitlaced, uptight, unresponsive. Therefore, when you think of *self-control* (the word I have chosen to translate *sophrosyne*) in Aristotle's sense, think of someone who knows his or her limits not only in a negative but also in a positive sense. Practicing *sophrosyne,* one knows not only how little but also how much one is capable of.

10. What is the nature of the pleasures associated with self-control and self-indulgence?

After courage, let us speak of self-control, for these two seem to be the virtues of the irrational parts of our nature.

We have already said that self-control is moderation or observance of the mean with regard to pleasures, for it is not concerned with pains as much as with pleasures, or in the same manner. Self-indulgence also presents itself in the same context.

Let us determine what kind of pleasures these are.

First let us accept as established the distinction between the pleasures of the body and the pleasures of the soul, such as the pleasures of fulfilled ambition or love of learning {which are pleasures of the soul}.

When he who loves honor or learning is delighted by what he loves, it is not his body that is affected, but his soul. But men are not called either self-controlled or self-indulgent for their behavior with regard to these pleasures; or for their behavior with regard to any other pleasures that are not of the body. For example, those who are fond of gossip and of telling stories, and spend their days in unimportant matters, are called gossips but not self-indulgent; nor do we apply this term to those who are extremely pained at the loss of money or friends.

Self-control, then, will be concerned with the pleasures of the body, but not even with all of these. Those who delight in the use of their eyesight, in colors and shapes and painting, are not called either self-controlled or self-indulgent. Yet it seems that it is possible to take delight in these things too as one should, and also more or less than one should, {and thus these things have a mean, excess, and deficiency}.

Other examples of pleasures of the body might be _____

_____

_____

_____.

1118a

It is the same with the sense of hearing: A man is never called self-indulgent for taking an excessive delight in music or in acting, or self-controlled for taking a proper delight in them.

Nor are these terms applied to those who delight, unless it be incidentally, in smells. We do not say that those who delight in the smell of fruit, roses, or incense are self-indulgent, but rather those who delight in the smell of perfumes and savory dishes. The self-indulgent man delights in these smells because they remind him of the things that he desires.

You may, indeed, see other people taking delight in the smell of food when they are hungry; but only a self-indulgent person takes excessive delight in such smells, as he alone is constantly desiring such things.

An example of taking "excessive delight " would be one who _____ _____ _____ _____.

The lower animals, moreover, do not get pleasure through these senses, except incidentally. It is not the scent of a hare that delights a dog, but the eating of it; only the presence of the hare comes through his sense of smell. The lion has no pleasure in the lowing of the ox, but in devouring him; but as the lowing announces that the ox is near, the lion appears to delight in the sound of it. So also, it is not seeing or discovering a stag or a wild goat that pleases him, but the anticipation of a meal.

Self-control and self-indulgence, then, have to do with those kinds of pleasure that are common to the lower animals, for which reason they seem to be slavish and bestial; I mean the pleasures of touch and taste.

Taste, however, seems to play only a small part here, or perhaps no part at all. For it is the function of taste to distinguish flavors, as is done by winetasters and by those who season dishes. It is by no means this kind of discrimination that gives delight to the self-indulgent but the actual enjoyment of them. {The enjoyment is always through}...the sense of touch in the pleasures of eating, drinking, and sexual intercourse. Hence a certain gourmet wished that his throat were longer than a crane's, thereby implying that his pleasure was derived from the sense of touch.

1118b
A gourmet might wish to have a throat longer than a crane's because _____ _____ _____!

That sense, then, with which self-indulgence is concerned is of all senses the commonest or most widespread among all living beings {i.e., the sense of touch}. Thus self-indulgence seems to be deservedly of all vices the most blamed, inasmuch as it attaches not to our human but to our animal nature.

To find one's delight in things of this kind, then, and to love them more than all things, is to be like an animal.

And further, the more manly kind of pleasures of touch, such as the pleasures that the gymnast finds in a rubdown and a warm bath, are excluded from the sphere of self-indulgence because the self-indulgent does not cultivate the sense of touch over his whole body, but only in certain parts.

Aristotle talks about the five senses in this section. What does he say about each, which two are closely connected to self-indulgence, and which of the two is most closely connected?

What Aristotle says about the pleasures of sight is _____

_____.

What he says about each of the other senses is: _____

_____

_____

_____

_____.

The two that are most closely connected to self-indulgence are

_____ because _____

_____.

Of these two the most significant is _____ because

_____.

11. What is the nature of self-control and its opposites?

Underline the differences between the self-controlled and the self-indulgent individual.

Now, of our desires or appetites some appear to be common to all men, others to be individual and acquired.

Thus the desire for food is natural or common to all men. Every man when he is in need desires meat or drink, or sometimes both, and sexual intercourse, as Homer says, when he is young and vigorous. But not all men desire to satisfy their appetites in this or that particular way, nor do all desire the same things; and therefore such desire appears to be unique to ourselves, or merely individual.

Of course it is also partly natural. Different people are pleased by different things, and yet there are some things that all men like better than other things.

Firstly, then, in the matter of our natural or common desires only a few men go wrong, and that only on one side, namely on the side of excess. For example, to eat or drink whatever is set before you until you can hold no more is to exceed what is natural in regard to quantity, because natural desire or appetite is simply for the filling of our needs. Thus, such people are called "belly-gorgers," implying that they fill their bellies too full. It is only those who are slaves to their desires that acquire this vice.

Secondly, with regard to those pleasures that are individual (i.e., that attend the gratification of our individual desires) many people go wrong in various ways.

People are called fond of this or that because they delight either in wrong things or in a wrong amount, as the masses do, or in a wrong way. Now, in all these ways those who are self-indulgent go to excess. They delight in some things in which they should not delight since they are detestable things, and if it is right to delight in any of these things, they delight in them more than is right, as the masses do.

It is plain, then, that excess in these pleasures is self-indulgence and is a thing to be blamed. But in regard to the corresponding pains the case is not the same here as it was with regard to courage. A man is not called self-controlled for enduring them, and self-indulgent for not enduring them; but the self-indulgent man is called self-indulgent for being more pained than he should at not getting certain pleasant things, his pain being caused by his loss of pleasure. The self-controlled man is called self-controlled because the absence of these pleasant things or the abstinence from them is not painful to him.

The words "these pleasures" refer to _____ _____ _____ .

1119a

The self-indulgent man, then, desires all pleasant things, or those that are most intensely pleasant, and is led by his desire to choose these in preference to all other things. Thus he is constantly pained by failing to get them and by desiring them, because all appetite involves pain; but it seems a strange thing to be pained for the sake of pleasure.

People who are deficient in regard to pleasure and take less delight than they should in these things are rarely found because this sort of insensitivity is not part of human nature. Indeed even the lower animals choose among different kinds of food and delight in some and not in others. A being to whom nothing was pleasant and who found no difference between one thing and another would be very far removed from being a man. We have no name for such a being because he does not exist.

The being who "does not exist" is _____ _____ .

But the self-controlled man observes the mean in these things. He takes no pleasure in those things that the self-indulgent most delights in—but rather rejects them—or generally in the wrong things, or very much in any of these things. When they are absent he is not pained, nor does he desire them, or desires them only moderately, not more than he should, at the wrong time, and so on. However, those things that are pleasant and at the same time lead to his health and bodily fitness he will desire moderately and in the right manner, and other pleasant things also, provided they are not injurious, incompatible with what is noble, or beyond his means. He who cares for these pleasures more than is proper differs from the self-controlled man, who is not apt to do that but is guided by right reason.

Some of the differences between the self-controlled and the self-indulgent individual are _____ _____ _____ _____ .

1119a20

Now, draw a portrait of the self-controlled individual in Aristotle's sense and compare this person with the way you saw a self-controlled individual before reading the *Nicomachean Ethics*.

Before reading Aristotle when I thought of someone who was self-controlled I thought of _____

_____.

The kinds of things this person would do would be _____

_____.

The main characteristics of a self-controlled person for Aristotle are _____

_____

_____.

Some characteristic actions of Aristotle's self-controlled person would be _____

_____.

The similarities and differences between my earlier view and Aristotle's are: _____

_____

_____.

Find one key description of the self-indulgent individual and then explain it.

Aristotle says, "_____

_____

_____."

Thus, a central characteristic of self-indulgence is _____

_____

_____.

Before going on to Book IV, we should have a brief review. Here is a list of questions about topics in Book III. Describe each briefly with or without looking back at your notes. The last four simply repeat chapter titles.

1. What are some samples of voluntary and involuntary actions?

_____

_____.

2. What is the difference between acting from choice and acting from wish?

_____

_____.

3. What are some of the differences between choice and opinion?

_____

_____.

4. What are some examples of things we can and cannot deliberate about?

_____

_____.

5. How does Aristotle solve the problem of the difference between wishing for the good and the apparent good?

_____

_____.

6. What is the nature of voluntary actions and our responsibility?

_____

_____.

7. What are some characteristics of courage and its opposites?

_____

_____.

8. What is the relationship between courage and pleasure and pain?

_____

_____.

9. What is the nature of the pleasures associated with self-control and self-indulgence?

_____

_____.

10. What is the nature of self-control and its opposites?

_____

_____.

Here is a problem to help guide your reading in the next chapter. Aristotle describes the virtue of generosity and its twin vices of excess and deficiency. Try to think of a word for each of those vices and characteristics of each of the three terms.

A generous person would be one who _____

_____.

If generosity was the mean, then the vice of excess might be called

_____ and it would be excessive

because _____

_____. The vice of deficiency would be called

_____ and it would be deficient

because _____.

Note the large number of examples Aristotle is able to use to describe these terms, especially generosity.

Book IV
Other Moral Virtues

Each of the next three chapters is an analysis of a virtue and its attendant vices of excess and deficiency. In Chapter 1 underline the key points Aristotle makes about generosity and its vices. Label these key points *G* for generosity, *E* for excess, and *D* for deficiency. This will simplify your writing task at the end of the chapter.

1. What are the characteristics of the virtue of generosity and the vices of extravagance and stinginess?

Generosity, of which we will next speak, seems to be moderation in the matter of wealth. What we praise in a generous man is his behavior, not in war, in those circumstances in which self-control is commended, or in passing judgment, but in the giving and taking of wealth, and especially in the giving—*wealth* meaning all those things whose value can be measured in money.

1119b21

Extravagance and stinginess are respectively excess and deficiency in regard to wealth.

Stinginess always means caring for wealth more than is right, but *extravagance* sometimes stands for a combination of vices. Thus morally weak people who squander their money in riotous living are called extravagant. And so those who are extravagant are held to be very worthless individuals as they combine a number of vices.

But we must remember that this is not the proper use of the term because the term *extravagant* is intended to denote a man who has one vice, namely that of wasting his wealth. He is extravagant who is destroyed through his own fault, and the wasting of one's wealth

1120a

is held to be a kind of destruction of one's self, as one's life is dependent on it. This, then, we regard as the proper sense of the term *extravagance.*

Anything that has a use may be used well or poorly. Riches is abundance of useful things. But each thing is best used by him who has the virtue that is concerned with that thing. Therefore he will use riches best who has the virtue that is concerned with wealth, that is, the generous man.

Now the ways of using wealth are spending and giving, while taking and keeping are the ways of acquiring wealth. And so it is more characteristic of the generous man to give to the right people than to take from the right source and not from the wrong source. It is more characteristic of virtue to do good to others than to have good done to you and to do what is noble than not to do what is base. Here it is plain that doing good and noble actions go with giving, while receiving good and not doing what is base go with taking.

Summarize each of Aristotle's points in the three following paragraphs beginning with

"Again".

Again, we are thankful to him who gives, not to him who does not take; and so we praise the former rather than the latter.

Again, it is easier not to take than to give because we are more inclined to be too stingy with our own goods than to take another's.

Again, it is those who give that are commonly called generous. Those who abstain from taking are not praised for their generosity especially, but rather for their justice. Those who take are not praised at all.

Again, of all virtuous characters the generous man is the most beloved, because he is helpful but his helpfulness lies in his giving. Virtuous acts, we said, are noble, and are done for the sake of that which is noble. The generous man, therefore, like the others, will give with a view to, or for the sake of, that which is noble and will give rightly; that is, will give the right things to the right persons at the right times. In short, his giving will have all the characteristics of correct giving.

Moreover, his giving will be pleasant to him, or at least painless because virtuous acts are always pleasant or painless—certainly very far from being painful.

He who gives to the wrong persons, or gives from some other motive than desire for that which is noble, is not generous but must be called by some other name.

Nor is he generous who gives with pain, because that shows that he would prefer the money to the noble action, which is not the feeling of the generous man.

The generous man, again, will not take money from the wrong sources because such taking is inconsistent with the character of a man who sets no store by wealth.

Nor will he be ready to beg a favor, because he who confers benefits on others is not usually in a hurry to receive them.

He will take from the right sources—for example, from his own property—not as if there were anything noble in taking but simply as a necessary condition of giving. Thus he will not neglect his property, since he wishes by means of it to help others. He will refuse to give to anybody and everybody, in order that he may have the necessary means to give to the right persons, at the right times, and where it is noble to give.

1120b
Underline the key characteristics of the generous individual.

It is very characteristic of the generous man to even go to excess in giving, so that he leaves too little for himself, because disregard of self is part of his character.

In applying the term *generosity* we must take account of a man's fortune, because it is not the amount of what is given that makes a gift generous but the generous habit or disposition of the doer. This disposition proportions the gift to the fortune of the giver. And so it is quite possible that the giver of the smaller sum may be the more generous man, if his wealth be smaller.

Those who have inherited a fortune seem to be more generous than those who have made one, because they have never known poverty, and all men are particularly fond of what they have made, as we see in parents and poets.

It is not easy for a generous man to be rich, because he is not likely to take or to keep but is likely to spend. He cares for money not on its own account but only for the sake of giving it away.

Hence the charge often brought against fortune is that those who most deserve wealth are least blessed with it. But this is natural enough because it is just as impossible to have wealth without taking trouble to get it as it is to have anything else.

Nevertheless the generous man will not give to the wrong people or at the wrong times, because if he did he would no longer be displaying true generosity and, after spending thus, would not have enough to spend on the right occasions. For, as we have already said, he is generous who spends in proportion to his fortune on proper objects, while he who exceeds this is extravagant. Thus rulers are not called extravagant, because the wealth is such that it does not seem easy for them to give away too much of it.

Generosity, then, being moderation in the giving and taking of wealth, the generous man will give and spend the proper amount on the proper objects, alike in small things and in great, and that with pleasure. He will also take the proper amount from the proper sources. For since the virtue is moderation in both giving and taking, the man who has the virtue will do both rightly. Right taking is consistent with right giving, but any other taking is contrary to it. Those givings and takings, then, that are consistent with one

Underline the key characteristics of the extravagant individual.

another are found in the same person, while those that are contrary to one another obviously are not.

If a generous man happens to spend anything in a manner contrary to what is right and noble, he will be pained, but moderately and in due measure; it is a characteristic of virtue to be pleased and pained on the right occasions and in the correct amount.

The generous man, again, is easy to deal with in money matters. It is not hard to cheat him, as he does not value wealth and is more likely to be unhappy at having failed to spend where he should than to be pained at having spent where he should not. He is the sort of man that Simonides[22] would not praise. The extravagant man, on the other hand, also errs in these points; he is not pleased or pained on the right occasions or in the right way, but this will be clearer as we go on.

We have already said that both extravagance and stinginess are at once excess and deficiency in two things, namely giving and taking, expenditure being included in giving. Extravagance exceeds in giving and in not taking but falls short in taking. Stinginess falls short in giving, but exceeds in taking—but only in small matters, we must add.

Now the two elements of extravagance are not commonly united in the same person: It is not easy for a man who never takes to be always giving because private citizens soon exhaust their means of giving, and it is to private citizens that the name is generally applied.

An extravagant man of this kind (i.e., in whom both the elements are combined), we must observe, seems to be better than a stingy man. For he {the extravagant man} is easily cured by advancing years and poverty and may come to the middle course because he has the essential aspects of the generous disposition. He gives and abstains from taking, though he does neither well or as he should. If then he can be trained to this, or if in any other way this change in his nature can be effected, he will be generous because then he will give to whom he ought and will not take where he should not. Thus he is generally thought not to be a bad person, because to go too far in giving and in not taking does not show a vicious or ignoble nature as much as a foolish one.

An extravagant man of this sort, then, seems to be much better than a stingy man, both for the reasons already given and because the former does good to many but the latter to no one, not even to himself.

The more extravagant individuals, as has been said, not only give wrongly but also take from wrong sources, and are in this respect stingy. They become grasping because they wish to spend but cannot readily do so because their resources soon fail. Thus they are compelled to draw from other sources. At the same time, since they care nothing for what is noble, they will take quite recklessly from any source whatever because they long to give but do not care how the money goes or where it comes from. *1121b*

Thus their gifts are not generous because they are not noble, nor are they given with a view to that which is noble or in the right manner. Sometimes they enrich those who should be poor and give nothing to men of respectable character, while they give a great deal to those who flatter them or provide them with any other pleasure. Thus most of them are self-indulgent because, being ready to part with their money, they are likely to lavish it on riotous living, and as they do not shape their lives with regard to that which is noble, they easily fall into the pursuit of pleasure.

The extravagant man, then, if he fails to find guidance, comes to this, but if he gets training, he may be brought to the moderate and right course.

Stinginess is incurable, however, because old age and all loss of power seem to make men stingy.

It also is more common than extravagance; the mass of men are more apt to be fond of money than of giving.

Again, it is far-reaching and has many forms because there seem to be many ways in which one can be stingy.

It consists of two parts—deficiency in giving and excess of taking—but it is not always found in its entirety. Sometimes the parts are separated, and one man exceeds in taking while another falls short in giving. Those, for instance, who are called by such names as close-fisted, stingy, and miserly, all fall short in giving but do not covet other people's goods or wish to take them.

Some are motivated by a kind of honesty or desire to avoid what is disgraceful. I mean that some of them seem, or at any rate profess, to be saving in order that they may never be compelled to do anything disgraceful, for example, the skinflint[23] (and those like him), who is so named because of the extreme lengths to which he carries his unwillingness to give.

Others are moved to keep their hands from their neighbors' goods only by fear, believing it to be no easy thing to take the goods of others without having one's own goods taken in turn. Thus they are content with neither taking nor giving.

Others, again, exceed in the matter of taking in order to make any gain they can in any way whatever, for example, those who ply debasing trades, brothel-keepers and similar people, and usurers who lend out small sums at a high rate. For all these make money from the wrong sources and more than they should. *1122a*

The common characteristic of these last seems to be the pursuit of petty gain. All of them endure blame for the sake of gain, and that is only a small gain. For those who make improper gains in improper ways on a large scale are not called stingy, for example,

Underline the key characteristics of stinginess.

tyrants who sack cities and pillage temples; they are called wicked, impious, unjust. The gambler, however, and the common thief are counted among the stingy because they make base gains. For example, both the thief and the gambler ply their trade and endure reproach for gain, and the thief for the sake of his booty endures the greatest dangers, while the gambler makes gain out of his friends, to whom he ought to give. Both then, wishing to make gain in improper ways, are seekers of base gain and all such ways of making money involve stinginess.

Thus, stinginess is rightly called the opposite of generosity because it is a worse evil than extravagance, and men are more apt to go wrong in this way than in that which we have described as extravagance.

Let this, then, be taken as our account of generosity and of the vices that are opposed to it.

Look back at your underlinings and labels *G, E,* and *D.* What were the key points Aristotle made about generosity, extravagance (the excess), and stinginess (the deficiency)? Support each of your assertions with a direct quotation and an original example.

About generosity, Aristotle says, "_____
_____." The point

he is making is _____
_____.

An example would be _____
_____.

An important point Aristotle makes about extravagance is "_____
_____
_____."

What he is saying is _____
_____.

This could be illustrated by _____
_____.

Describing stinginess he says, "_____
_____
_____."

In essence, he means _____
_____.

I remember once when _____
_____
_____.

    Now do the same thing in the next chapter. Underline key parts of Aristotle's discussion of magnificence, gaudiness, and pettiness and label them with *M*, *V*, and *P* respectively.

2. What are the characteristics of magnificence, gaudiness, and pettiness?

Our next task seems to be an examination of magnificence in spending. For this also seems to be a virtue that is concerned with wealth.

    But it does not, like generosity, extend over the whole field of financial transactions but only over those that involve large expenditure, and in these it goes beyond generosity in amount. For, as its very name suggests, it represents suitable expenditure on a grand scale. But the grandness is relative: The expenditure that is suitable for a man who is fitting out a warship is not the same as that which is suitable for the head of a sacred embassy.

    What is suitable, then, is relative to the person, the occasions, and the object of expenditure. Yet he who spends what is fitting on insignificant or moderately important occasions is not called magnificent. For example, the man who can say, in the words of the poet,

    To many a wandering beggar did I give;

{is not magnificent}, but he is who spends what is fitting on great occasions. The magnificent man is generous, but a man may be generous without being magnificent.

    The deficiency of this quality is called pettiness; the excess of it is called gaudiness. The characteristic of the latter is not spending too much on proper objects, but spending ostentatiously on improper objects and in improper fashion. We will speak of these in a few moments.

    The magnificent man is like a skilled artist; he can see what a situation requires, and can spend great sums tastefully. As we said at the start, a disposition is defined by the acts that produce it and the things it produces.

    The magnificent man's expenses, therefore, must be large and appropriate {to the occasion}.

The way in which a person could be generous without being

magnificent is if _____
_____
_____
_____.

1122b

What he produces, then, will also be of the same nature, because it is only in this way that the expense will be at once large and suitable to the result.

The result, then, must be worthy of the expense and the expense proportionate to the result or even greater.

Moreover, the magnificent man's motive in thus spending his money will be desire for that which is noble, because this is the common characteristic of all the virtues.

Further, he will spend gladly and lavishly because exact accounting of cost is ignoble. He will inquire how the work can be made most beautiful and most elegant, rather than what its costs will be or how it can be done most cheaply.

The magnificent man must be generous also because the generous man is one who will spend the right amount in the right manner…. Magnificence is distinguished from generosity (which has the same sphere of action) by greatness—I mean by actual magnitude of amount spent. Secondly, where the amount spent is the same, the result of the magnificent man's expenditure will be more splendid.

Now there is a kind of expenditure that is called praiseworthy, such as expenditure on the worship of the gods, for example, offerings, temples, and sacrifices. Also all expenditure on the worship of heroes and all public service that is prompted by a noble ambition are praiseworthy. For example, a man may think it proper to furnish a chorus {for a play} or a warship or to give a public feast in a grand style.

But in all cases, as we have said, we must regard the person who spends, and ask who he is, and what his means are. Expenditure should be proportionate to means, and be suitable not only to the result but also to the persons who spend.

Thus a poor man cannot be magnificent. He does not have the wealth to spend large sums suitably. If he tries, he is a fool because he spends disproportionately and in a wrong way; an act must be done in the right way to be virtuous. Magnificence is becoming in those who have the necessary means, either by their own efforts or through their ancestors or by their connections. They also should have the proper parents and reputation. All these things give a man a certain greatness and importance.

The magnificent man, then, is a man of this sort, and magnificence exhibits itself most properly in expenditure of this kind, as we have said because this is the greatest and most honorable kind of expenditure. It may also be displayed on private occasions such as the kind that occur but once in a man's life, for example, a wedding or anything of that nature. Or {grand expenditures can be made} when they are of special interest to the state or the governing classes, for example, receiving strangers and sending them on their

A good example of Aristotle's "magnificent man" in the modern world would be _____ _____ because _____ _____ _____ _____ _____ .

1123a

way or making presents to them and returning their presents. The magnificent man does not lavish money on himself but on the common good....

Again, a magnificent man will build his house in a style suitable to his wealth because even a fine house is a kind of distinction. And he will spend money more readily on things that last because these are the noblest.

He will provide what is appropriate for each occasion, which is not the same for gods as for men, for a temple as for a tomb. In his expenditure every detail will be appropriately great, great expenditure on a great occasion being the most magnificent. In other situations he will spend whatever is great for that occasion.

Again, the greatness of the result is not the same as the greatness of the expense. For example, the most beautiful ball or the most beautiful bottle that can be found is a magnificent present for a child, though its price is small.

This, then, is the character of the magnificent man.

The man who goes too far, whom we call a vulgarian, exceeds, as we said, in spending improperly. He spends great sums on little objects and makes an inappropriate display. For example, if he is entertaining a few friends, he will give them a wedding feast; if he provides the chorus for a comedy, he will bring his company on-stage all dressed in royal purple, as they {ostentatiously] do in Megara. And all this he will do from no desire for what is noble or beautiful but merely to display his wealth, because he hopes to gain admiration, spending little where he should spend much, and much where he should spend little.

But the petty man will fall short on every occasion and, even when he spends very large sums, will spoil the beauty of his work for a trifle, never doing anything without thinking twice about it, considering how it can be done at the least possible cost, bemoaning even that, and thinking he is doing everything on a needlessly large scale.

Both these dispositions, then, are bad but they do not bring reproach, because they are neither injurious to others nor very offensive in themselves.

The difference between the magnificent individual and the vulgarian is that the former _____ _____ _____ while the latter _____ _____ _____.

You know what to do.

One of the first important points Aristotle makes about the magnificent man is "_____ _____." In essence he is saying _____ _____.

An example of a magnificent action in the Aristotelian sense would be _____

_____ .

Aristotle describes gaudiness as "_____

_____ ."

Putting this into my own words, _____

_____ .

An appropriate example would be _____

_____ .

One of his most accurate observations about pettiness is his view that "_____

_____ ."

His point is _____

_____ .

An example of this aspect of pettiness would be _____

_____ .

In the next chapter, we find one of the more difficult terms to translate: *megalopsychia*. Literally, this means "greatness of soul," and it has been translated as *high minded, magnanimous,* and *aristocratically proud.* Try to keep in mind these last three translations when you encounter references to greatness of soul in the next chapter. To make matters more difficult Aristotle contrasts *megalopsychia* with *mikropsychia*, which is literally "smallness of soul." This has been translated as *pettiness, small minded,* and *pusillanimous.* Keep these three in mind when you read about smallness of soul. The great-souled individual is one of the stars of the *Nicomachean Ethics.* Aristotle mounts to no higher praise until the last chapters when he describes the life of contemplation.

To focus your reading of this crucial chapter, try to describe what someone would be like who could be called great souled, high minded, magnanimous, and aristocratically proud.

When I think of someone like this I see the image of someone

who _____ .

The kinds of actions a great-souled individual would perform would be _____

_____ .

Someone who was great-souled or magnanimous would be happy when _____

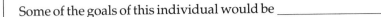

Some of the goals of this individual would be _____

_____

_____.

My opinion of such a person would be _____

_____

_____.

Underline examples of greatness of soul, vanity, and smallness of soul and label each *G, S,* and *V* respectively.

3. What are greatness of soul, vanity, and smallness of soul?

Greatness of soul seems from its very name to have to do with great things; let us first determine what these are.

It will make no difference whether we consider the quality {of greatness of soul} itself, or the man who exhibits the quality.

By a great-souled man we seem to mean one who claims much and deserves much. He who claims much without deserving it is a fool, but the possessor of a virtue is never foolish or silly. The man we have described, then, is great-souled.

1123b

He who deserves little and claims little is modest but not great-souled. Greatness of soul implies greatness just as beauty implies stature; small men may have appeal and be well proportioned but cannot be called beautiful.

He who claims much without deserving it is vain, though not everyone who claims more than he deserves is vain.

He who claims less than he deserves is small-souled. Whether what he deserves is great, moderate, or small, he claims still less. But the fault seems to be greatest in him who deserves a great deal, because what would he do if what he deserved was less than what it is?

The great-souled man, then, in regard to the greatness of what he deserves occupies an extreme position, but he behaves as he should, and observes the mean because he claims what he deserves, while all others claim too much or too little.

An example of a "great-souled" individual in the modern world

would be _____

_____

because _____

_____

_____

_____.

If he deserves much and claims much, and most of all deserves and claims the greatest things, there will be one thing with which he will be especially concerned. (What one deserves has reference to external good things.) Now the greatest of external good things we may assume to be what we render to the gods as their due, what people in high stations most desire, and what is the reward appointed for the noblest deeds. But the thing that answers to this

Underline the key characteristics of the great-souled individual on this and the following three pages.

description is honor, which, we may safely say, is the greatest of all external goods. Honors and dishonors, therefore, are the field in which the great-souled man behaves as he should.

And indeed we may see, without going to the trouble of proving it, that honor is what great-souled men are concerned with, because it is honor that great men claim and deserve.

The small-souled man falls short, whether we compare his claims with what he deserves or with what the great-souled man claims for himself.

The vain or conceited man exceeds what is due to himself, though he does not exceed the great-souled man in his claims.

The great-souled man, as he deserves the greatest things, must be a perfectly good or excellent man, because the better man always deserves the greater things, and the best possible man the greatest possible things. The really great-souled man, therefore, must be a good or excellent man. And indeed greatness in every virtue or excellence seem to be necessarily implied in being great-souled.

It would be equally inconsistent with the great-souled man's character to run away in battle or to commit an act of injustice, because he has no real reason to act basely. There is nothing he loves enough to commit injustice for, because all things are of little account to him.

Consider him aspect by aspect and you will find that the notion of a great-souled man who is not a good or excellent man is absurd. Indeed, if he was not good, he would not be worthy of honor, because honor is the prize of virtue and is rendered to the good as what is proper to them.

1124a

Greatness of soul, then, seems to be the crowning grace, as it were, of the virtues. It makes them greater, and cannot exist without them. Because of this it is a hard thing to be truly great-souled; or, to put it another way, it is impossible without the union of all the virtues.

The great-souled man, then, exhibits his character especially in the matter of honors and dishonors. When he receives great honors from good men he will be moderately pleased, as he will be getting nothing more than what he deserves, or even less because no honor can be adequate to complete virtue. Nevertheless he will accept it, as they have nothing greater to offer him. But honor from ordinary men and on trivial grounds he will utterly despise because that is not what he deserves. Dishonor likewise he will reject because he never merits it.

But though it is especially in the matter of honors, as we have said, that the great-souled man displays his character, he will also observe the mean in his feelings with regard to wealth and power and all kinds of good and evil fortune, whatever may happen to him. He will not be very much exalted by prosperity, or very much cast down by adversity, because not even honor affects him as if it were a very important thing. Since power and wealth are desirable for honor's sake, at least those who have them wish to gain honor by them, he who thinks lightly of honor must think lightly of them also.

Thus, great-souled men seem to look down upon everything.

The gifts of fortune also are commonly thought to contribute to greatness of soul. For those who are wellborn are thought worthy of honor, and also those who are powerful or wealthy. They are in a position of superiority, and that which is superior in any good thing is always held in greater honor…. But strictly speaking it is only the good man that is worthy of honor, though he that has both goodness and good fortune is commonly thought to be more worthy of honor. However, those who have these good things without virtue do not have any just claim to great things, nor should they be called great-souled, because neither is possible without complete virtue.

Those who have these good things easily become haughty and insolent. Without virtue it is not easy to bear the gifts of fortune gracefully, and so, being unable to bear them and thinking themselves superior to everybody else, such people look down on others and do whatever happens to please them. They imitate the great-souled man without being really like him and do this whenever possible. They do not exhibit virtue in their acts {as a great-souled man would}, but they look down on others {in the same way as a great-souled man}. Only the great-souled man never looks down on others without justice, for he estimates others correctly while most men do so for quite irrelevant reasons.

The great-souled man is not quick to run into petty dangers and indeed does not love danger, since there are few things that he greatly values; but he is ready to incur a great danger, and whenever he does so is reckless with his life, as a thing that is not worth keeping at all costs.

It is his nature to confer benefits, but he is ashamed to receive them because the former is the role of a superior, the latter of an inferior. And when he has received a benefit, he is likely to confer a greater in return. In this way his creditor will become his debtor and be in the position of a recipient of his favor.

It is thought, moreover, that such men {the great-souled} remember those on whom they have conferred favors better than those from whom they have received them. The reason is that the recipient of a benefit is inferior to the benefactor, but such a man {the great souled} wishes to be in the position of a superior. Thus, he likes to be reminded of the one but dislikes to be reminded of the other. This is the reason we read that Thetis would not mention to Zeus the services she had done him, and why the Lacedaemonians, in dealing with the Athenians, reminded them of the benefits received by Sparta rather than of those conferred by her.

Some characteristics of a great-souled individual thus far are:

1. _____

_____

2. _____

_____

3. _____

_____

4. _____

_____ .

1124b

It is characteristic of the great-souled man, again, never or reluctantly to ask favors, but to be ready to confer them and to be lofty in his behavior to those who are high in station and favored by fortune but affable to those of the middle ranks. It is a difficult, a dignified thing to assert superiority over the former but easy to assert it over the latter. A haughty demeanor in dealing with the great is quite consistent with good breeding, but in dealing with those of low estate it is crude, like showing off one's strength on a cripple.

Another of his characteristics is not to rush wherever honor is to be won, or to go where others take the lead, but to hold aloof and to shun an enterprise, except when great honor is to be gained or a great work is to be done. He does not do many things but only great and notable things.

Again, he must be open in his hate and in his love, for concealment shows fear.

He must care for truth more than for what men will think of him, and {thus he will} speak and act openly. He will not hesitate saying all that he thinks, since he looks down on mankind. Thus he will speak the truth except when he speaks ironically, and irony he will employ in speaking to the masses of men.

1125a

Another of his characteristics is that he cannot shape his life to suit another, unless the other is a friend, because that {shaping your life to suit others} is slavish. So all flatterers of great men are of a slavish nature, and men of low natures become flatterers.

Nor is he easily moved to admiration because nothing appears great to him.

He easily forgets insults because it is not consistent with his character to brood on the past, especially on past wrongs, but rather to overlook them.

Additional characteristics of a great-souled individual are:

1. _____

_____

2. _____

_____

3. _____

_____

4. _____

_____ .

He is no gossip. He will not talk about himself or about others because he does not care that men should praise him, or that others should be blamed, though, on the other hand, he is not very ready to bestow praise. Thus, he is not likely to speak evil of others, not even of his enemies, except to scorn them.

When an event happens that cannot be helped or is of slight importance, he is the last man in the world to cry out or beg for help because that {crying out} is the conduct of a man who thinks these events very important.

He loves to possess beautiful things that bring no profit, rather than useful things that pay because this is a characteristic of the man whose wealth is in himself.

Further, the character of the great-souled man seems to require that his gait should be slow, his voice deep, his speech deliberate. A man is not likely to be in a hurry when there are few things in which he is deeply interested, or excited when he holds nothing to be of very great importance: These are the causes of a high voice and rapid movements.

This, then, is the character of the great-souled man.

But he that is deficient in this quality is called small-souled; he that exceeds vain.

Now these two also do not seem to be bad—for they do no harm—though they are in error.

The small-souled man, though he deserves good things, deprives himself of what he deserves, and so seems worse off for not claiming these good things and for misjudging himself. If he judged correctly, he would desire what he deserves as is proper. I do not mean to say that such people seem to be fools, but rather they are too self-depreciating. But a misjudgment of this kind does seem actually to make them worse because men strive for what they deserve and shrink from noble deeds and employments of which they think themselves unworthy, as well as from mere external good things.

But vain men are fools as well as ignorant of themselves and make this plain to all the world. Not doubting their worth they undertake honorable offices for which they are not qualified. They dress in fine clothes, put on fine airs, and so on; they wish everybody to know their good fortune; they talk about themselves as if that were the way to honor.

But littleness of soul is more opposed to greatness of soul than vanity is because it is both commoner and worse. Greatness of soul, then, as we have said, has to do with honor on a large scale. *1125a35*

Now summarize Aristotle's view of the great-souled and the small-souled man.

Aristotle's clearest description of the great-souled man is

"_____

_____."

To paraphrase, _____

_____.

A modern example would be someone who _____

_____.

A small-souled man is one who "_____

_____."

To put this in other words, _____

_____.

A clear example of this kind of person is _____

_____.

Aristotle illustrates vanity, the vice of excess, by saying, "_____

_____."

My own way of putting this would be _____

_____.

Picture someone who _____

_____.

Let us think more about Aristotle's description of virtue and vice in this chapter. About smallness of soul he says, "The small-souled man, though he deserves good things, deprives himself of what he deserves, and so seems worse off for not claiming these good things and for misjudging himself." In some sense small-ness of soul sounds like humility, which, because of the Christian values of our culture, we think of as virtuous. And, on the other hand, there are aspects of the great-souled man that appear to us to be simply arrogant. Go back through your underlinings and, from your own point of view, list the positive and negative characteristics of the great-souled individual. Then make your judgment.

Positive characteristics	Negative characteristics

When I look at the great-souled individual, I see someone who _____

_____

_____.

Book V
Justice

Summary

(No selections from Book V are included in this edition of the *Nicomachean Ethics;* the following is a brief summary.)

1129a–1138b15

Aristotle begins Book V by distinguishing universal justice from particular justice. Universal justice concerns what is lawful, while particular justice concerns what is fair and equal. Particular justice is itself divided into two kinds: distributive and rectificatory. Distributive justice proceeds in accordance with geometrical proportion, while rectificatory justice proceeds in accordance with arithmetical progression. Distributive justice divides honors according to merit, while rectificatory justice has to do with awarding damages or rectifying a wrong that has been done.

In the latter portions of Book V Aristotle examines various meanings of the term *justice.* The most important aspect of these sections involves the relationship between "voluntary action" and "just" or "unjust" action. Aristotle's main point is that justice is not simply a way of acting but a disposition, a quality of personality.

Book VI
Intellectual Virtues

Book VI begins a new topic for the *Nicomachean Ethics:* intellectual virtues. Moral virtues like courage, self-control, and generosity were the major subject of the first four books; the two major intellectual virtues are theoretical and practical wisdom.

Moral virtues involve the correct control of our feelings, and intellectual virtues involve the correct exercise of our reason. In Book VI Aristotle indicates that we can use our reason in two "virtuous" ways: We can reason correctly about matters of everyday life and thus possess practical wisdom, or we can reason correctly about scientific or philosophical matters and thus possess theoretical wisdom. Aristotle's way of putting this is to say that theoretical wisdom involves things that cannot be other than what they are and practical wisdom involves things that can be other than what they are. In other words, the scientist and the philosopher study the permanent structures of the universe that are as they have to be and cannot be changed by human action. Practical wisdom, the second intellectual virtue, takes the realm of daily life as its object. Exercising practical wisdom, we control all the parts of our lives that we can control. We plan, deliberate, choose among options. Both practical and theoretical wisdom involve the use of reason. In the case of the former, reason correctly exercised solves life's problems; in the case of the latter, reason correctly exercised penetrates the riddles of the cosmos.

There are no pedagogical aids, except titles in the form of questions, in the following selections from Book VI, and there are none in Book VII except at the end of the final chapter. Practice

the skills you developed in the first four books; underline important points and make your own notes slowly and wisely in the
margins.

1.   What are the parts of the soul?

We said above that what we should choose is neither too much nor   *1138b17*
too little but the intermediate, and that the intermediate is what
right reason prescribes. This we now have to explain.

Each of the virtues we have discussed implies, as every mental
habit implies, some aim that the rational man keeps in view when
he is regulating his actions; in other words, there must be some standard for determining the kinds of moderation, which we say lie
between excess and deficiency and are in accordance with right reason. But though this is quite true, it is not sufficiently precise. In
any kind of occupation that can be reduced to rational principles,
it is quite true to say that we must exert ourselves and relax ourselves neither too much nor too little, but in moderation, as right
reason orders. But this alone would not tell one much. For example, a man would hardly learn how to treat a case by being told
to treat it as the art of medicine prescribes and as one trained in that
art would treat it.

So in the case of dispositions it is not enough that the rule we
have laid down is correct. We need also to know precisely what this
right reason is and what its standard is.

The virtues of the soul, it will be remembered, we divided into
two classes and called the one moral and the other intellectual. The
moral virtues we have already discussed in detail. Let us now   *1139a*
examine the other class, the intellectual virtues, after some prelimi-
nary remarks about the soul.

We said before that the soul consists of two parts, the rational
and the irrational part. We will now make a similar division of the
former, and will assume that there are two rational faculties: (1) that
by which we know those things that cannot be other than what they
are, (2) that by which we know those things that can be other than
what they are. Different faculties {like the two rational faculties}
must study correspondingly different subjects {like (1) and (2) above}
if, as we hold, it is because of some kind of likeness with their
subjects that our faculties are able to know them.

Let us call the former the scientific {the correct exercise of which
involves theoretical wisdom}, the latter the calculative faculty {the
correct exercise of which involves practical wisdom}. For to deliberate is the same as to calculate, and no one deliberates about things
that cannot be other than what they are. One division then of the
rational faculty may be justly called the calculative faculty.

Our problem, then, is to find what each of these faculties becomes in its full development, or in its best state, because that will be its excellence or virtue.

But its excellence will bear direct reference to its proper function.

12. What is the use of theoretical and practical wisdom?

Here an objection may be raised. "What is the use of them {theoretical and practical wisdom}?" it may be asked. Theoretical wisdom does not consider what tends to make man happy, for it does not ask how anything is brought about, {it only studies things as they are}. Practical wisdom indeed does this, but why do we need it? Practical wisdom is the faculty that deals with what is just and noble and good for man, that is, with those things that the good man does. However, the knowledge of them does not make us more able to do them. {For example}, a knowledge of medicine and gymnastics does not make us more able to do these things {because knowing what is good in any particular case does not guarantee we will do what is good}.

And if it is meant that a man should have practical wisdom, not in order that he may know what these {good and noble} actions are, but in order that he may do them, then practical wisdom will be no use to those who are {already} good or even to those who are not. For it will not matter whether either of these kinds of individuals have practical wisdom themselves or take the advice of others who have it. It will be the same in these matters as in regard to health; if we wish to be in health, we do not go and learn medicine.

Again, it seems to be a strange thing that practical wisdom, though inferior to theoretical wisdom, must yet govern it, since in every field the practical faculty guides and issues orders.

We must discuss these points; just now we have been only stating objections.

First of all, then, we say that both practical wisdom and theoretical wisdom must be desirable in themselves, since each is the virtue of one of the parts of the soul, even if neither of them produces anything.

Next, they do produce something.

On the one hand, theoretical wisdom produces happiness, not in the sense in which medicine produces health, but in the sense in which health produces health; that is to say, theoretical wisdom being a part of complete virtue, its possession and exercise make a man happy. {The possession and exercise of theoretical wisdom *is* the highest form of happiness; see the final chapters of Book X.}

On the other hand, in the sphere of action man performs his function perfectly when he acts in accordance with both practical wisdom and moral virtue, because while the latter ensures the rightness of the end aimed at, the former ensures the rightness of the means to that end....

But as to the objection that practical wisdom makes us no more apt to do what is noble and just, let us take the matter a little deeper, beginning this way—

We agree, on the one hand, that some who do just acts are not yet just, for example, those who obey the laws either involuntarily or through ignorance, or for some external motive and not for the sake of the acts themselves, even though they do what they should and all that a good man should do. And, on the other hand, it seems that when a man does these acts with a certain disposition he is good; that is, when he does them as a result of deliberate choice, and for the sake of the acts themselves.

Now, the rightness of the choice is secured by {moral} virtue, but to decide what should be done in order to carry out the choice belongs not to {moral} virtue but to another faculty. But we must dwell a little on this faculty and try to make it quite clear.

There is a faculty that we call cleverness—the power of hitting upon and carrying out the means that lead to any proposed goal. If the goal is noble, the faculty {cleverness} merits praise; but if the end is base, the faculty is the faculty of the evildoer. Thus we apply the term *clever* both to the man of practical wisdom and the evildoer.

Now this power is not identical with practical wisdom, but is its necessary condition. But this power, the "eye of the soul" as we may call it, does not attain its perfect development without moral virtue, as we said before, and may be shown thus: All syllogisms or deductive reasonings about what is to be done have for their starting point {principle or major premise} "the end or the supreme good is so and so" (whatever it be; any definition of the good will do for the argument). But it is only to the good man that this presents itself as the good because vice perverts us and causes us to go wrong about the principles of action. So it is plain, as we said, that it is impossible to have practical wisdom without being morally good.

13. What is the relationship between practical wisdom and moral virtue?

...some people say that all the virtues are forms of practical wisdom,   *1144b17*
and in particular Socrates held this view, being partly right in his
inquiry and partly wrong—wrong in thinking that all the virtues

are actually forms of practical wisdom, but right in saying that they are impossible without practical wisdom....

It is evident, then, from what has been said that it is impossible to be good in the full sense without practical wisdom, or to have practical wisdom without moral virtue. In this way we can meet one objection that might be presented. "The virtues," it may be said, "are found apart from each other; a man who is strongly predisposed to one virtue does not have an equal tendency toward all the others, so that he will have acquired this virtue while he still lacks that." We may answer that though this may be the case with some virtues, yet it cannot be the case with those virtues for which we call a man good without any qualifying epithet. The presence of the single virtue of practical wisdom implies the presence of all the moral virtues.

And thus it is plain, in the first place, that even if it had no bearing on action, we should still need practical wisdom as the virtue or excellence of a part of our soul; and, in the second place, {it does have a bearing on action because} choice cannot be right without both practical wisdom and moral virtue because the latter makes us desire the end, while the former makes us adopt the right means to the end.

Nevertheless, practical wisdom does not rule theoretical wisdom and the better part of our nature {the reason}, any more than medicine is the ruler of health. Practical wisdom does not employ theoretical wisdom in its service, but provides means for the attainment of theoretical wisdom—does not rule it, but rules in its interests. To say the contrary would be like saying that statesmanship rules the gods, because it issues orders about all public concerns {including the worship of the gods}.

Book VII
Moral Strength and Weakness

> The first three chapters of Book VII are important to Aristotle's ethical analysis but are, unfortunately, awkwardly organized. Aristotle's topic is moral strength and weakness. In Chapter 1 he presents six current beliefs about moral strength and weakness and then in the next chapter, in no clear order, raises problems about some of these current beliefs. In the Chapter 3 he solves some of the problems he raised in Chapter 2. Following Martin Ostwald, I have numbered each of the current beliefs and then numbered the references to these beliefs in the two succeeding chapters. There is no easy way to read Chapters 2 and 3 except to keep turning back to the current beliefs he is referring to in Chapter 1.
>
> No pedagogical aids are included so that you can test your powers of analysis against some of the most difficult material in the *Nicomachean Ethics*.

1. What is the nature of moral strength and weakness?

…we will now speak of moral weakness, softness, and luxuriousness, and also of moral strength and hardiness, for we must regard these as the names of characteristics that are neither identical with virtue and vice respectively nor yet generically different {but part of the same class}. *1145a35*

Here we must follow our usual method, and, after stating the current opinions about these characteristics, proceed first to raise objections, and then to establish, if possible, the truth of all the *1145b* current opinions on the subject, or, if not of all, at least of the greater number and the most important. If the difficulties can be resolved and the current beliefs confirmed, we will have achieved as much certainty as the subject allows.

It is commonly thought (1) that moral strength and hardiness are good and laudable, while moral weakness and softness are bad and blamable; (2) that a morally strong man is identical with one who abides by his calculations, and a morally weak man with one who swerves from them; and (3) that the morally weak man, knowing that an act is bad, is impelled to do it by passion, while the morally strong man, knowing that his desires are bad, is withheld from following them by reason. Also (4) it is said that the self-controlled man is morally strong and tenacious: But some hold this is true and others think it is not always so; and while some people hold that the self-indulgent man is morally weak and that the morally weak man is self-indulgent, and use these terms indiscriminately, others make a distinction between them. Again (5), with regard to the man who has practical wisdom, sometimes people say it is impossible for him to be morally weak; at other times they say that some men who have practical wisdom and are clever are morally weak. Lastly (6), people are called morally weak even in regard to anger and the pursuit of honor and profit.

2. What are some of the problems involved with current beliefs about moral strength and weakness?

But in what sense, it may be objected, can a man judge rightly when he acts from moral weakness? {See (3).}

Some people maintain that a man cannot do anything but act rightly if he really knows what is right because Socrates thought it would be strange if, when a man possess knowledge, something else should control him and drag him about like a slave. Indeed, Socrates disagreed with the whole position, maintaining that there is no such thing as moral weakness: When a man acts contrary to what is best, he never, according to Socrates, has correct knowledge about the case, but acts from ignorance.

Now this theory {of Socrates} evidently conflicts with experience {where we observe people who have correct knowledge but who make morally weak choices}; {we should instead investigate} the passion that sways the morally weak man; if it really is due to ignorance, we must ask what kind of ignorance it is due to. For it is plain that he who acts from moral weakness knows his action is wrong until he is swayed by his passion.

There are other people who in part agree and in part disagree with Socrates. They agree that nothing is able to prevail against knowledge, but do not agree that men never act contrary to what seems best. They say that the morally weak man, when he yields to pleasure, does not have knowledge but only opinion.

Again {see 4}, if a man cannot be morally strong without having strong and bad desires, the self-controlled man will not be morally strong, or the morally strong man self-controlled, because it is incompatible with the self-controlled disposition to have either very violent or bad desires.

1146a

The desires must, however, be both strong and bad in the morally strong man. For if they were good, the habit that hindered him from following them would be bad, so that moral strength would not be always good; if they were weak and not bad, it {moral strength} would be nothing to respect; {nor would moral strength be something to respect} if they were bad, but at the same time weak.

Again {see (1) and (2)}, if moral strength makes a man likely to abide by any opinion whatsoever, it is a bad thing—for example, if it makes him abide by a false opinion. And if moral weakness makes a man likely to abandon any opinion whatsoever, there will be a kind of moral weakness that is good. An example would be Neoptolemus in the *Philoctetes* of Sophocles. He merits praise for being prevented from persevering in the plan that Ulysses had persuaded him to adopt by the pain that he felt at telling a lie.

Again {see (1) and (3)}, the well-known argument of the Sophists, though fallacious, creates a difficulty. Wishing to establish a paradoxical conclusion, so that they may be thought clever if they succeed, they construct a syllogism that puzzles the hearer because his reason is fettered, as he is unwilling to accept the conclusion, which is unsatisfactory to him, but he is unable to advance, since he cannot find a weakness in the argument. Thus it may be argued {as the Sophists do} that folly combined with moral weakness is virtue: {the argument is that} by reason of his moral weakness a man does the opposite of what he judges to be good; but he judges that the good is bad and not to be done; the result is that he will do the good and not the bad.

1146a30

Something of this sort, then, are the objections that suggest themselves; and of these we must remove some and leave others; for the resolution of a difficulty is the discovery of the truth.

[1146a31–1146b7] *of VII 2 omitted.*

3. What are the solutions to some problems involved with moral weakness and knowledge?

We have, then, to inquire (1) whether the morally weak man acts with knowledge or not, and what *knowledge* means here; then (2)

1146b8

what is to be regarded as the situations in which moral strength and moral weakness occur—I mean whether their manifestations involve all pleasures and pains or only certain definite classes of these; then (3), with regard to the morally strong and the tenacious man, whether they are the same or different; and so on with the other points that are related to this inquiry.... Let us now turn to question (1) {in this chapter}.

As to the argument that it is true opinion and not knowledge that the acts of morally weak men violate, it really makes no difference here because some of those who merely have opinions are in no doubt at all but believe that they have exact knowledge.

If then it is said that those who have opinion more readily act against their judgment because of the weakness of their belief {in the opinion}, we would answer that there is no such difference between knowledge and opinion, because some people have just as strong a belief in their mere opinions as others have in what they really know; Heraclitus[24] is an example.

But, in fact, we use the word *know* in two different senses: He who has knowledge that he is not now using is said to know a thing, and also he who is now using his knowledge. Therefore, having knowledge that is not now present to the mind about what one should not do will be different from having knowledge that is now present. Only in the latter sense, not in the former, does it seem strange that a man should act against his knowledge.

Again, since these reasonings involve two kinds of premises, a universal proposition for the major and a particular for the minor, there is nothing to prevent a man from acting contrary to his knowledge though he has both premises, if he is now using the universal only and not the particular, because the particular is the thing to be done.

Again, different kinds of universal propositions may be involved: One may concern the individual himself, another the thing. For example, you may reason (1) "all men are benefited by dry food, and this is a man"; and (2) "This kind of food is dry"; but the second minor premise, "this particular food is dry," may be unknown or the knowledge of it may be dormant.

These distinctions, then, will make a vast difference, so much so that it does not seem strange that a man should act against his knowledge if he knows in one way, though it does seem strange if he knows in another way.

But it is possible for a man to "have knowledge" in yet another way than those just mentioned. We see, I mean, that "having knowledge without using it" includes different modes of having, so that a man may have it in one sense and in another sense not have it. For example, a man who is asleep, mad, or drunk {has knowledge in one sense but not another}. People who are being swayed by a passion are in a similar state because anger, sexual desire, and similar emotions do evidently alter the condition of the body and in some cases actually produce madness. It is plain, then, that the morally weak man {only} has knowledge in the same sort of way as those who are asleep, mad, or drunk.

To repeat the words of knowledge is no proof that a man really has knowledge, in the full sense of having an effective knowledge, because even when they are under the influence of these passions people repeat mathematical demonstrations and sayings of Empedocles, just as students string words together before they understand their meaning. The meaning must be ingrained in them, and that requires time. Thus, we must hold that the morally weak repeat words in the same sort of way that actors do.   *1147a25*

It seems that what Socrates sought to establish really is the case;[25]   *1147b15*
for when passion carries a man away, what is present to his mind is not what is regarded as knowledge in the strict sense, nor is it such knowledge that is perverted by his passion {but the kind of dormant knowledge we have just been describing}.   *1147b19*

One of the central problems in Greek ethics is whether a person can do a wrong action knowing beforehand that it is wrong. Socrates held that this was impossible because people never knowingly do harm to themselves, and doing a wrong action is self-harming. From Socrates' point of view, if I were an alcoholic and I took a drink, I would do this wrong, harmful action because I did not really know that it was harmful. What is your view? Is it possible to *fully* know something is wrong and do it anyway?

1. If you say it is possible, you have to show how someone could choose what they know is a choice that will bring them pain.

2. If you say it is not possible, you have to explain in what sense a person like an alcoholic does not know that his or her actions will be harmful.

Try thinking like Aristotle who often presents good arguments for positions he later refutes. First, argue as strongly as you can for (1), then argue as strongly as you can for (2); then show which of the two arguments is the best and why. Use the example of the alcoholic in each argument.

The strongest argument I can make for (1) in the case of an

alcoholic would be _____

_____

_____ .

But one could also argue for (2) in the example of an alcoholic and

say _____

_____

_____.

Now I will have to offer an additional argument to show which

of the two, (1) or (2), is stronger. My view is _____

_____

_____.

Here is one more puzzle. Does Aristotle agree with Socrates
or not?

The answer is _____.

Prove it.

Aristotle says "_____

_____." The

point is _____.

Which of the two arguments does Aristotle support?

He supports _____.

Why?

Near the end of this chapter he makes the following points:

_____

_____

_____.

Thus, using the example of the alcoholic, his conclusion would be

in the case of argument (1) and (2) _____

_____

because _____

_____.

In the next book Aristotle begins an investigation of friendship. Test yourself against him. Present several good reasons
why we need friends.

Very well. _____

_____

_____

_____.

Now underline Aristotle's reasons for needing friends in the
opening sections of Book VIII.

Book VIII
Friendship

1. Why do we need friends?

After the foregoing, a discussion of friendship will naturally follow, as it is a sort of virtue, or at least implies virtue, and is, moreover, necessary to our lives. No one would care to live without friends though he had all other good things. Indeed, it is when a man is rich and has power and authority that he seems to need friends the most. What is the use of all his prosperity if he has no opportunity for benevolence, which is most frequently and commendably displayed toward friends? How could his position be maintained without friends? The greater his position is, the more it is exposed to danger. In poverty and all other misfortunes we regard our friends as our only refuge. We need friends when we are young to keep us from error and when we get old to take care of us and to carry out those plans that we do not have strength to carry out ourselves. In the prime of life we need friends to help us in noble deeds—"two together," as Homer says—because thus we are more efficient both in thought and in action.

Friendship seems to be implanted by nature in the parent toward its offspring, and in the offspring toward its parent, not only among men, but also among birds and most animals; {it also seems to be implanted by nature} in those of the same race toward one another, among men especially. For this reason we praise those who love their fellowmen. And when one travels abroad one may see how man is always akin to and dear to man.

Again, it seems that friendship is the bond that holds states together and that lawgivers are even more eager to secure it than justice. Concord bears a certain resemblance to friendship, and it is

1155a

Some important points made thus

far about friendship are: _____

_____

_____

_____

_____

_____ .

1155b

1155b3

1155b15

concord that lawgivers especially wish to retain and dissension that they especially wish to banish as an enemy. If citizens are friends, they have no need for justice, but even if they are just, they also need friendship or love; indeed the most complete realization of justice seems also to be the most complete realization of friendship.

Moreover, friendship is not only an indispensable but also a beautiful or noble thing. We commend those who love their friends, and having many friends is a noble thing. Some even think that a good man has the same characteristics as a friend.

There are several differences of opinion about friendship. Some hold that it is a kind of likeness, and that those who are like one another are friends. This is the origin of "Like to like," "Birds of a feather flock together," and other similar sayings. Others, on the contrary, say that "two of a trade never agree."

Others go deeper into these questions and into the causes of the phenomenon; Euripides, for instance, says

> The parched Earth loves the rain, and the high heaven, with moisture laden, loves Earthward to fall.

Heraclitus also says, "Opposites fit together, " "Out of discordant elements comes the fairest harmony," and "It is by battle that all things come into the world." Others, notably Empedocles, take the opposite view that like desires like.

Of these difficulties, all that refer to the structure of the universe may be dismissed, for they do not properly concern our present inquiry; but those difficulties that refer to human nature and are intimately connected with man's character and affections, we will discuss—for example, whether friendship can exist in all men, or whether it is impossible for men to be friends if they are bad. We will also consider whether there is one kind of friendship or many. Those who suppose that there is only one kind of friendship, because it admits of degrees, are wrong. Things that differ in kind may differ also in degree.

In the first paragraph Aristotle presents reasons why different kinds of people need friends. He also discusses several other major topics related to friendship. Go back over this chapter, draw a line across the page each time he begins a new subject; in essence, you will be dividing the chapter into its logical units. What are they?

After rereading I can see there are _____ logical units or

subtopics in this chapter. They are _____

_____

_____ .

He mentioned one subject in this chapter just to say he will not look into it further.

That is _____. The reason

he will not deal with it is _____

_____.

In the next two chapters, the chapter titles give you obvious clues about what to underline.

2.   What are the three things worthy of affection?

Perhaps these difficulties will be cleared up if we first determine what is the object worthy of affection. For it seems that we do not feel affection for anything but the lovable and that the lovable is either good, pleasant, or useful. But *useful* appears to mean whatever helps us to get something good or some pleasure; thus only the good and the pleasant would be worthy of affection as ends.

Now, do men love what is good in general, or what is good for themselves? There is sometimes a discrepancy between these two and also in the case of what is pleasant.

It seems that (1) each man loves what is good for himself, and that while the good is lovable in itself, each man finds lovable what is good for him. It may be said that (2) each man loves not what is really good for him, but what seems good for him. But this will make no difference, for (3) the lovable we are speaking of will then be the apparently lovable. The motives of love are thus threefold.

The love of inanimate things is not called friendship because there is no return of affection or any wish for the good of the object. It would be absurd to wish well to wine, for example; at the most, we wish that it may keep well in order that we may have it. But it is commonly said that we must wish our friend's good for his own sake. One who thus wishes the good of another is called a well-wisher when the wish is not reciprocated; when the well-wishing is mutual, it is called friendship.

1155b34

Simple question. The three things worthy of affection are?

Simple answer. The first is _____.

The second is _____. The third

is _____.

Near the end of the following section Aristotle says, "Is there only one kind of friendship, or are there more than one?"

As you might imagine, Aristotle will find several kinds of friendship, three to be exact. His analysis is based on the different kinds of things friends do for each other. As you also might guess, he ranks the kinds of friendship and finds one kind clearly superior to the others. Try to do the same thing.

Very well. Thinking about my own life, I will try to divide my friendships into three groups, and then rank and describe each. I will start at the highest. The best kind of friendship involves _____

_____

_____.

In this kind of relationship what one friend does for another is

_____

_____.

A second kind of friendship involves _____

_____.

What one friend does for another is _____

_____.

This is less satisfactory than the first kind because _____

_____.

The third kind of friendship involves _____

_____.

What each friend does for the other is _____

_____.

This is the least satisfactory kind of friendship because _____

_____.

In the following chapter on the three kinds of friendship evaluate the strengths and weaknesses of Aristotle's argument. In general his analysis is likely to be better than yours. Try to see why. There are also some weak places in his argument; note those as well and we will discuss your evaluation following this unit.

3. What are the three kinds of friendship?

Number each of the three kinds of friendship.

Now those who love one another wish each other's good based on the motive of their love. Those, therefore, whose love for one another is based on the useful do not love each other for what they are but only in so far as each gets some good from the other.

It is the same also with those whose affection is based on pleasure; people care for a wit, for instance, not for what he is but as the source of pleasure to themselves.

Those, then, whose love is based on the useful care for each other on the basis of their own personal good, and those whose love is based on pleasure care for each other on the basis of what is pleasant to themselves, each loving the other, not as being what he is, but as useful or pleasant.

These friendships, then, are only incidentally friendships. The object of affection is loved, not as being the person that he is, but as the source of some good or some pleasure. Friendships of this kind, therefore, are easily dissolved, as the persons do not remain unchanged, because if they cease to be pleasant or useful to one another their love ceases. The useful is nothing permanent but varies from time to time. On the disappearance, therefore, of what was the motive of their friendship, the friendship itself is dissolved, since it existed solely for its usefulness.

Some friendships are easily

dissolved because _____

_____

_____

_____.

Friendship of this kind seems especially to be found among elderly men (for at that time of life men pursue the useful rather than the pleasant) and those middle-aged and young men who have a keen eye to what is profitable. Friends of this kind do not generally even live together because sometimes they are by no means pleasant, nor indeed do they want such constant intercourse with others unless they are useful. They make themselves pleasant only as far as they have hopes of getting something good as a result.

The kind of friendship that exists between host and guest is generally this kind of friendship.

The friendship of young men seems to be based on pleasure. Young men live by impulse and, for the most part, pursue what is pleasant to themselves and whatever the moment brings. But the things in which they take pleasure change as they advance in years. They are quick to make friendships, therefore, and quick to drop them. Their friendship changes as the object that pleases them changes; pleasure of this kind is liable to rapid change.

Moreover, young men are apt to fall in love because love is, for the most part, a matter of impulse and based on pleasure. Thus they fall in love, and again soon cease to love, passing from one state to the other many times in one day.

1156b

Friends of this kind wish to spend their time together and to live together because thus they attain the object of their friendship.

The perfect kind of friendship, however, is that of good men who resemble one another in virtue. They both wish well to one another as good men, and it is their essential character to be good men. Those who wish well to their friends for the friends' sake are friends in the truest sense; their attitude toward their friends is determined by their friends' true nature and not by incidental aspects of that nature. Their friendship, therefore, lasts as long as their virtue, and virtue is a long-lasting thing.

Again, each is both good in an unqualified way and good to his friend, because it is true of good men that they are both good in an unqualified way and also beneficial to one another. For similar reasons, they are pleasant, too, because good men are both pleasant in themselves and pleasant to one another....

This kind of friendship, then, is lasting, as we might expect, since it unites in itself all the conditions of true friendship. Every friendship has for its motive some good or some pleasure whether it be in itself or relative to the person who feels the affection. Every friendship also implies some similarity between the friends. In the present case these qualities are present in the character of both friends. The two friends are similar to each other and the good and pleasant are present in the relationship.... Thus, it is between persons of this sort that the truest and best love and friendship are found.

It is natural that such friendships should be rare because such people are rare. Such a friendship, in addition, requires time and familiarity. As the proverb says, it is impossible for people to know one another until they have consumed the necessary quantity of salt together. Nor can they accept one another as friends or be friends until each shows himself to the other as worthy to be loved. Those who quickly come to treat one another like friends may wish to be friends but are not really friends, unless they not only are worthy of affection but also know each other to be worthy of affection. A wish to be friends may come quickly, but not friendship.

[1156b33–1163b2] in Bk 8 omitted.

Some of the characteristics of the highest kind of friendship are: _____

_____

_____

_____

_____

_____

1156b32

What are the three kinds of friendship?

They are: _____

_____. The main characteristics of the first are: _____

_____. The main characteristics of the second are: _____

_____. The main characteristics of the third are:

_____

_____.

Try to apply Aristotle's analysis to your own life.

When I divide my past and present friends into these three kinds of groups what I see is _____

_____

_____.

What are the strongest and weakest parts of Aristotle's argument?

The strongest part of Aristotle's analysis is _____

_____ because _____

_____. The weakest part is _____

_____ because _____

_____. Of everything

he says in this section, one of the wisest things is "_____

_____."

He means _____

_____. This is wise because

_____

_____.

Book IX
Analysis of Friendship Continues

The selections we will look at from this book are full of practical advice about friendship. In Chapter 3 Aristotle discusses the dissolution of friendships, in Chapter 9 he considers the relation between self-love and friendship, in Chapter 10 he presents the practical problem of the number of friends one should have. One of the peculiarities of the history of philosophy is that the greatest minds often do not bother trying to solve problems of daily life. No one but Aristotle has tried to determine the proper number of friends, and this is one of his small glories.

In the following chapter Aristotle addresses four practical questions. The first question is: Should a friendship be broken off when the friend does not remain who he was, that is, when one friend changes?

One of the best arguments for breaking off the friendship would be _____
_____.

One of the best arguments against breaking off the friendship would be_____
_____.

My own view is _____
_____ because _____
_____.

Now analyze what Aristotle says.

[1163b28–1165a3b] omitted from Bk 9.

3. What are the reasons for dissolving a friendship?

Another difficult question is whether we should break off friendship with those who have ceased to be what they were.

1165b

We may, perhaps, say that those whose friendship is based on profit or pleasure naturally part when these {profit and pleasure} cease because it was these that they loved. When these are gone, therefore, it is to be expected that the love goes too. But complaints would be likely to arise if a man who loved another for profit or pleasure's sake pretended to love him for his character. As we said at the outset, quarrels between friends very frequently arise from a difference between the real and the supposed motives of the friendship. If, then, a man deceives himself and supposes that he is loved for his character, though the other's behavior gives no ground for the supposition, he has only himself to blame. But if he is deceived by the other's pretense, then there is a good reason for complaint against such an impostor, even more than against those who counterfeit coinage, inasmuch as it {friendship} is a more precious thing that is tampered with.

An example of what Aristotle is talking about in this section would be two friends who _____ _____ _____ _____ _____.

In essence, Aristotle has two answers to the question whether it is right to break off a friendship when one friend changes. It depends, as one might suppose, on the kind of friendship.

The kind of friendship it is right to break off when one friend

changes is _____ because _____
_____.

The point he makes about the other kind of friendship, which it

would not be right to break off, is _____
_____.

Looking at the difference between his answer and mine, I see

_____
_____.

Think about a similar case. Let us say one friend became wicked; would it be right to break off the friendship?

I would say _____ because _____
_____.

And also because _____
_____.

Here is Aristotle's answer.

But if a man becomes friends with someone he believes to be a good man, and the new friend becomes and shows himself to be a bad man, is he still to be loved? Perhaps we may answer that it is impossible, as it is not everything that is lovable but only the good. A bad man, then, is not lovable and ought not to be loved, for we should not love what is bad, or make ourselves similar to what is worthless. And, as we said before, it is like that makes friends with like.

Is the friendship, then, to be immediately broken off? Perhaps not in all cases, but only in the case of those who are incurably bad. When it is possible to reform them, we are more bound to come to the aid of their character than to their property, because character is a nobler thing, and has more to do with friendship than property. But a man who withdraws his friendship in such a case seems to do nothing unnatural, for it was not with such a man that he made friends. His friend has become another man, and as he cannot save him, he stands apart from him.

An example of a friendship of this sort that should not be broken off would be _____ _____ _____ _____.

1165b23

omitted [1166b24–1168a28]

What were the main points Aristotle made?
  The condition under which it is not right to break off a relationship with a friend who has become wicked is when _____ _____ because _____ _____.

Otherwise one should _____ because _____.

  Next consider the case when one friend becomes far superior to the other. Should or could the friendship be maintained? For example, say one friend has grown up and the other remains "mentally a child."
  My view is _____ because _____.

But suppose that the one remains what he was while the other gets better and becomes far superior in virtue: Is the latter still to treat the former as a friend? Perhaps it is hardly possible that he should do so. We see this most plainly if the difference between the two is very great. Take, for instance, a boyhood friendship: If one of the two remains mentally a child, while the other has become a man in the fullest sense of the word, how can they any longer be friends now that the things that will please them and the sources of their joys and sorrows are no longer the same? For not even in regard to each other will their tastes agree, and without this, we found, people cannot be friends, since they cannot live together. But this point has been already discussed.

Aristotle's essential point was?

_____

_____ .

You can see in this chapter how carefully Aristotle considers even the smallest philosophical problem. In terms of daily life, however, these problems about friends are not small problems at all. Now, should a former friend be treated as if he was never a friend at all?

I hope Aristotle says _____ because

I believe _____ .

Shall we, then, simply say that the latter {the one who became mature} should regard the former {the one who remained immature} as a stranger just as if they had never been friends? Perhaps we may say that he should not entirely forget their former relationship, and that just as we hold that we should serve friends before strangers, so former friends have some claims on us on the basis of past friendship, unless extraordinary wickedness was the cause of our parting.

Note how Aristotle continues to give "mixed" answers. In one sense we ought to treat former friends decently; however, there is a consideration that might change our attitude.

First Aristotle says, "_____

_____ ." He finishes, however, by

pointing out _____ .

My own view is _____ .

What I would like to remember from this chapter is _____

_____ .

We will look carefully at the next section, Chapter 8, in Appendix A: "Writing a Short Essay about Aristotle." For now, read it slowly, underline important points, and make your own margin notes. Once more note how practical and detailed Aristotle's advice is. Look for "mixed" answers; in this chapter he will point out when self-love is noble and when it is not.

8. Should we love ourselves more than we love others?

1168a29

Underline examples of when self-love is and is not good.

Another question that is raised is, should we love ourselves more than others?

We blame, it is said, those who love themselves most, and apply the term *self-loving* to them as a term of reproach. And, again, he who is not good is thought to think of himself in everything that he does, and the worse he is, the more he thinks of himself. Thus, we accuse him of doing nothing without self-interest. On the other hand, it is thought that the good man takes what is noble as his motive, and the better he is the more he is guided by this motive and, out of regard for his friend, neglects his own interest.

1168b

But this theory disagrees with facts, nor is it surprising that it does, for it is agreed that we should love him most who is most truly a friend. He is most truly a friend who, in wishing well to another, wishes well to him for his, the other's, sake, even though no one should ever know this. But all these characteristics, and all the others that go to make up the definition of a friend, are found in the highest degree in a man's relations to himself. We have already seen how it is from our relations to ourselves that all our friendly relations to others are derived. Moreover, all the proverbs point to the same conclusion—such as "Friends have one soul," "Friends have all things in common," "Equality makes friendship," "Charity begins at home." All these characteristics are found in the highest degree in a man's relations to himself, because he is his own best friend. Thus he must love himself better than anyone else.

People are not unnaturally puzzled to know which of these two positions {loving ourselves more or loving others more} to adopt, since both appeal to them.

Perhaps the best method of dealing with conflicting statements of this kind is to analyze them and clearly distinguish how far and in what sense each is right. So here, if we first determine what *self-loving* means in each statement, the difficulty will perhaps be cleared up.

Those who use *self-loving* as a criticism apply the name to those who take more than their share of money, honor, and bodily pleasures, because the mass of men desire these things and set their hearts on them as the best things in the world, so they are keenly competed for. Those, then, who grasp at more than their share of these things indulge their animal appetites and their passions generally—in a word, the irrational part of their nature. This is the character of the mass of men and hence the term *self-loving* has come to be used in this bad sense from the fact that the greater part of mankind are not good. It is with justice, then, that we find fault with those who are self-loving in this sense.

It can be easily shown, that it really is to those who take more than their share of these things that the term is usually applied by the mass of men. If what a man always set his heart on were that he rather than another should do what is just, temperate, or in any other way virtuous—if, in a word, he were always claiming the noble course of conduct, no one would call him self-loving, and no one would find fault with him.

And yet such a man seems to be more truly self-loving. At least he takes for himself what is noblest and most truly good and satisfies the ruling power {of reason} in himself and in all things obeys it. But just as the ruling part in a state or in any other system seems more than any other part to be the state or the system {itself}, so also the ruling part of a man seems to be most truly the man's self. Therefore, he who loves and satisfies this part of himself is most truly self-loving.

Again, we call a man morally strong or morally weak, based on whether his reason has the ruling part, implying that his reason is the same as himself. When a man has acted under the guidance of his reason, he is thought, in the fullest sense, to have done the deed himself and of his own will.

It is plain, then, that this part of us is our self, or is most truly our self, and that the good man more than any other loves this part of himself. He, then, more than any other, will be self-loving, in another sense than the man whom we fault as self-loving, differing from him by all the difference that exists between living according to reason and living according to passion, between desiring what is noble and desiring what appears to be profitable.

Those who more than other men set their hearts on noble deeds are welcomed and praised by all. But if all men were competing with each other in the pursuit of what is noble and were straining every nerve to act in the noblest possible manner, the result would be that the needs of the community would be perfectly satisfied, and at the same time each individual would achieve virtue, which is the greatest of all good things.

The good man, therefore, ought to be self-loving, because by doing what is noble he will at once benefit himself and others. The bad man should not {be self-loving} because he will injure both himself and his neighbors by following passions that are not good.

Thus with the bad man there is a discrepancy between what he should do and what he does, but with the good man what he should do is what he does because reason always chooses what is best for itself, and the good man obeys the voice of reason.

Again, it is quite true to say of the good man that he does many things for the sake of his friends and his country and will even die for them, if need be. He will throw away money, honor, and, in a

Continue to underline examples of when self-love is and is not good.

The words "this part" refer to _____
_____.

1169a

word, all the good things for which men compete, claiming the noble for himself. He will prefer a brief period of intense pleasure to a long period of mild pleasure, one year of noble life to many years of ordinary life, one great and noble action to many little ones. This, we may perhaps say, is what he gets who gives his life for others. Thus, he chooses for himself something that is noble on a grand scale.

Such a man will surrender wealth to enrich his friend, for while his friend gets money, he gets what is noble. In this way he takes the greater good for himself.

His conduct will be the same with regard to honors and offices. He will give up all to his friend because he believes this is noble and praiseworthy.

Such a man, then, is not unreasonably considered good, as he chooses what is noble in preference to everything else.

But, again, it is possible to give up to your friend an opportunity for action, and it may be nobler to cause your friend to do a deed than to do it yourself.

It is plain, then, that in all cases in which he is praised the good man takes for himself a larger share of what is noble. And in this sense, as we have said, a man ought to be self-loving, but not in the sense in which the mass of men are self-loving.

1169b

> As I said, we will discuss this section in detail later on the tour. In the next section Aristotle answers the question, "How many friends should we have?" What do you think?
>
> My view is _____ because _____
>
> _____ .
>
> I have selected four paragraphs (labeled A, B, C, and D) in the following for you to read carefully. At the end of the chapter write a title for each and summarize its argument.

Ch. 9 [1169b2–1172a15] omitted.

10.   How many friends should we have?

1170b20

Are we to make as many friends as possible? Or shall we say that in the case of friendship it is best neither to be friendless nor yet to have too many friends?

{A} With regard to friends who are chosen with a view to being useful, the latter idea seems to be perfectly appropriate. It would be troublesome to repay the services of a large number {of friends}, and

Key points in {A}?

_____

_____

_____ .

indeed life is not long enough to enable us to do it. Of such friends, therefore, a larger number than is sufficient for one's own life would be superfluous and a hindrance to noble living; so we do not want more than that number.

Again, of friends chosen with a view to pleasure a small number is enough in the same way that a small amount of sweets is enough in our diet.

{B} But are we to have as many *good men* for friends as we can, or is there any limit of numbers in friendship, as there is in a state? You could not make a state out of ten men, and if you had a hundred thousand your state would cease to be a state. But perhaps the right number of citizens is not one fixed number but any number within certain limits. And so with friends there is a limit to their number, and that is, we may say, the largest number that one can live with because living together is, as we saw, one of the most essential characteristics of friendship, and it is quite evident that it is impossible to live with and spread one's self among a large number.

Moreover, a man's friends must be friends with one another, if all are to spend their time together; but this is difficult with a large number.

{C} Again, it becomes hard for a man to sympathize duly with the joys and sorrows of a large number, because then he is likely to have at the same time to rejoice with one and to grieve with another. Perhaps, then, the best plan is not to try to have as many friends as possible but only as many as are sufficient for a life in common. Indeed it would be impossible to have an ardent friendship with a great number.

And, for the same reason, it is impossible to be in love with many persons at once because it seems being in love is a sort of superlative friendship, and that is only possible toward one person. Similarly, a close friendship is possible with only a few people.

{D} And this seems, in fact, to happen: We do not find a number of people bound together by the sort of friendship that exists between comrades, and the friendships that the poets celebrate are friendships of two persons. The man of many friends, who is friends with everybody, seems to be really friends with no one in any other way than as fellow citizens are friends—I mean the man we call obsequious.

Having friends as fellow citizens, indeed, it is possible to be friends with a great number and yet not be obsequious but a truly good man. The kind of friendship that is based on virtue and on regard for the friend's self one cannot have for many, but one must be well satisfied if one can find even a few such persons.

[1171a22–1172a15] omitted.

Key points in {B}?
_____
_____
_____.

1171a

Key points in {C}?
_____
_____
_____
_____.

Key points in {D}?
_____
_____
_____
_____.

What would be a good title for each of the four key paragraphs and how would you summarize the main ideas of each?

Very well. A good title for paragraph A would be _____
_____.

In essence, it says _____
_____.

A good title for paragraph B would be _____
_____
_____.

The main idea is _____
_____.

A good title for paragraph C would be _____
_____.

Aristotle's main point is _____
_____.

A good title for paragraph D would be _____
_____.

In essence, Aristotle says _____
_____.

Book X
Pleasure and Happiness

1. What are the two views of pleasure?

Our next business, I think, should be to describe pleasure. For pleasure seems, more than anything else, to have an intimate connection with our nature. This is the reason why in educating the young we use pleasure and pain as rudders to guide their course. Moreover, delight in what we should delight in and hatred of what we should hate seem to be of primary importance in the formation of a virtuous character, because these feelings pervade the whole of life and have power to draw a man to virtue and happiness, as we choose what pleases and avoid what pains us.

The discussion of these matters is especially necessary because there is much dispute about them. There are people who say that the good is pleasure, and there are people who say on the contrary that pleasure is altogether bad—some, perhaps, in the conviction that it is really so, others because they think it has a good effect on men's lives to assert that pleasure is a bad thing, even though it is not. The mass of men, they say, are slaves to their pleasures, so that they should be pulled in the opposite direction because thus they will be brought into the middle course.

But I do not think this is right. Assertions about matters of feeling and conduct carry less weight than actions. Thus, when assertions are found to be at variance with obvious facts, these assertions are rejected, and also discredit the truth. When a man who speaks against pleasure is seen at times to desire it himself, he appears to show by the fact of being attracted by it that he really considers all pleasure desirable, because the mass of men are not able to draw fine distinctions. It seems, then, that true statements

1172a16
Underline the two views of pleasure.

1172b

are more useful for practice as well as for theory. Being in harmony with the facts, they gain credence and so incline those who understand them to guide their lives by them. But enough of this: Let us now go through the current opinions about pleasure.

1172b8

> Aristotle begins a new topic, the discussion of pleasure. He indicates there are two attitudes toward pleasure; one that it is good and another that it is bad (logically enough). He refutes some proponents of the second. Who are they and how does he refute them?
>
> They are the ones who hold _____
>
> _____ and he
>
> points out _____
>
> _____.

In the next chapter Aristotle presents Eudoxus' view that pleasure is the supreme good. In other words, pleasure is the end of all ends. According to this view, once we have pleasure, we want nothing else from life. This seems convincing. Note how Aristotle presents this argument in Chapter 2A and then attacks it in Chapter 2B.

2A. What is Eudoxus' view of pleasure?

1172b9

Eudoxus' reasons for holding

pleasure is the good are: _____

_____

_____

_____

_____

_____.

Eudoxus[26] thought pleasure was the good because he saw that all beings, both rational and irrational, strive after it; but in all cases, he said, what is desirable is good, and that which is most desirable is best. The fact, then, that all beings tend toward the same thing indicates that this is the best thing for all, because each being finds out what is good for itself—its food, for instance. Thus what is good for all and that all strive after is the {chief} good.

The statements of Eudoxus were accepted because of the excellence of his character rather than for their own value, for he seemed to be a remarkably self-controlled man. People believed that it was not from love of pleasure that he believed as he did but that what he said really was true.

Eudoxus also thought that his point could be proved no less clearly by the argument from the opposite of pleasure: {This argument is} pain is in itself an object of aversion for all beings; therefore its opposite, pleasure, is desirable for all.

Again, he argued that something is most desirable if we choose it for its own sake and not for the sake of something else. But this is agreed to be the case with pleasure because we never ask a man for his motive in seeking pleasure, because we understand that pleasure is in itself desirable.

Aristotle presented three of Eudoxus' arguments for the view that pleasure is the chief good. Put them into your own words.

The first argument is _____

_____.

The second argument is _____

_____.

The third argument is _____

_____.

Now, Aristotle presents a fourth argument and then refutes it. After reading the following section, write a title for it.

2B.

Again, he argued that any good thing is made more desirable by the addition of pleasure, for example, just or temperate conduct; but it can only be by the good that the good is increased.

Now, this last argument seems indeed to show that pleasure is a good thing, but not that it is any better than any other good thing, because any good thing is more desirable with the addition of another good thing than by itself.

Plato actually employs a similar argument to show that pleasure is not the {chief} good. "The pleasant life," he says, "is more desirable with wisdom than without: But if the combination of the two is better, pleasure itself cannot be the good because no addition can make the good itself more desirable." And it is equally evident that, if any other thing be made more desirable by the addition of one of the class of things that are good in themselves, that thing cannot be the {chief} good. What good is there, then, that is thus incapable of addition, and at the same time such that men can participate in it? That is the sort of good that we want.

"He" is _____.

1172a34

What is the fourth argument Aristotle presents supporting Eudoxus' view that pleasure is the chief good and how does Aristotle use an argument by Plato to refute Eudoxus? In effect, Aristotle uses Plato's version of Eudoxus' argument to refute Eudoxus.

Eudoxus held that _____

_____.

Plato's version of this argument was that _____

_____

_____.

Thus, Eudoxus is used to refute Eudoxus because _____

_____.

Your only task in the next section is to write a good title.

2C.

Those who maintain, on the contrary, that what everyone desires is not good, surely talk nonsense. What everyone believes to be true must be true. And to him who bids us put no trust in the opinion of mankind, we reply that we can hardly put greater trust in his opinion. If it were merely irrational creatures that desired these things, there might be something in what he says; but as rational beings also desire them, how can it be anything but nonsense? Indeed, it may be that even in inferior beings there is some natural principle of good stronger than themselves that strives after their proper good.

Again, what the adversaries of Eudoxus say about his argument from the nature of the opposite of pleasure, does not seem to be sound. They say that, though pain be bad, yet it does not follow that pleasure is good because one bad thing may be opposed to another bad thing, and both to a third thing that is different from either. Now, though this is not a poor argument, it does not hold true in the present instance. For if both were bad, both alike ought to be rejected, or if neither were bad, neither should be rejected, or at least one no more than the other. But, as it is, men evidently reject the one as bad and choose the other as good. Therefore, they are in fact opposed to one another in this respect.

[1173a14–1176a29]

In the next three chapters selected from Book X Aristotle returns to the topic of happiness that he began with in the early chapters of Book I. In the following chapter he summarizes several of his important conclusions about happiness and shows how happiness is not the same thing as "pleasant amusements." Underline the most important parts of his argument and put them in your own words in the margins.

6. What is happiness?

Now that we have discussed the several kinds of virtue, friendship, and pleasure, all that remains is to give a summary of happiness, since we assume that it is the end or goal of all human actions. It will simplify our task if we first recapitulate what we said before.

1176a30

We said that happiness is not a state {permanently attached to an individual}. If it were, it would be within the reach of a man who slept all his days and lived the life of a vegetable, or of a man who met with the greatest misfortunes. As we cannot accept this conclusion, we must define happiness as some kind of activity, as we said before. But as some activities are sometimes necessary and only desirable for the sake of something else, other activities are desirable in themselves. It is evident that happiness must be placed among those that are desirable in themselves, and not among those that are desirable for the sake of something else. For happiness lacks nothing; it is sufficient in itself.

1176b

Now, an activity is desirable in itself when nothing is expected from it beyond itself.

Of this nature are held to be (1) the manifestations of virtue, because to do what is noble and excellent must be counted desirable for itself, and (2) those amusements that please us, because they are not chosen for the sake of anything else—indeed men are more apt to be injured than to be benefited by them through neglect of their health and fortunes.

Now most of those whom men consider happy indulge in pastimes of this sort. For this reason those who are skilled in such pastimes find favor with tyrants because they make themselves pleasant in providing what the tyrant wants, and what he wants is amusement. These amusements, then, are generally thought to be elements of happiness, because people in power employ their leisure in them. But such persons, we may venture to say, are no criterion. For high rank does not guarantee the possession of virtue or of reason, which are the sources of all excellent exercise of our faculties. And if these men, never having tasted pure and refined pleasure, have recourse to the pleasures of the body, we should not because of that think these more desirable, because children also believe that the things that they value are better than anything else. It is only natural, then, that as children differ from men in their estimate of what is valuable, so bad men should differ from good.

As we have often said, therefore, what is truly valuable and pleasant is what is so to the man of good character. Now the exercise of those trained faculties that are proper to him is what each man finds most desirable. What the man of good character finds most desirable, therefore, is the exercise of virtue.

Examples of "these amusements" might be _____

_____

_____

_____

_____ .

The reason happiness does not

consist in amusement is _____

_____

_____

_____ .

1177a

Other reasons why happiness is not

amusement are: _____

_____

_____ .

1177a11

Happiness, therefore, does not consist in amusement; indeed it is absurd to suppose that the end {of life} is amusement and that we toil all our life long for the sake of amusing ourselves. We might say that we choose everything for the sake of something else excepting only happiness because it is the end {of all ends}. But to be serious and to labor for the sake of amusement seems silly and utterly childish, while to play in order that we may be serious, as Anacharsis says, seems to be right. Amusement is a sort of recreation, and we need recreation because we are unable to work continuously.

Recreation, then, cannot be the end because it is taken as a means to the exercise of our faculties.

Again, the happy life is thought to be one that exhibits virtue, and such a life must be serious and cannot consist in amusement.

Again, it is held that things of serious importance are better than laughable and amusing things, and that the better the organ or the man, the more important is the function. But we have already said that the function or exercise of what is better is higher and more conducive to happiness.

Again, the enjoyment of bodily pleasures is within the reach of anybody, of a slave no less than the best of men; but no one supposes that a slave can participate in happiness, seeing that he cannot participate in the proper life of man. For indeed happiness does not consist in pastimes of this sort, but in the exercise of virtue, as we have already said.

What was Aristotle's strongest argument against the view that happiness is the same thing as amusement, or as we might say, leisure activities?

He says, "_____

_____ ."

His point is _____

_____ . My own

view is _____

_____ .

Remember his view is that happiness, true happiness, involves completely realizing the human function. When we are actualizing what is best and most distinctive about humans, then we will be truly happy. What is most distinctive about humans is our reason, and the highest use of our reason, Aristotle argues, involves philosophical contemplation. (Thus he might argue that your progress through this book has been a journey toward the highest happiness!)

It might be easiest for you to evaluate Aristotle's arguments in the next two chapters if you drew a portrait of ideal human activity. What is the best or noblest thing any individual can do with his or her life? A Christian might present someone like Saint Francis as a model of the highest human type. Thus, obeying God and serving the poor would be the noblest human activity. A Marxist might argue that a revolutionary is the ideal human type; creating revolution and redistributing wealth would be the noblest and most fulfilling human activity. In the last few years many have followed the banner of "be all you can be." Develop your self-confidence. Be assertive. Love yourself first so that you can be more loving to others. Under this view, the greatest thing a person can do is realize his or her own *unique* potential. (Note how Aristotle argues that we all have the *same* highest potential—the use of our reason in contemplation of philosophical truths.)

Make your own portrait of the perfect human type. Then describe what this person would do and whether these activities would produce happiness. Start with a concrete example. Finish by giving yourself some good advice.

When I think of all the people I have known or heard about, the one individual who seems to represent the ideal human is

_____. I choose this person because

_____

_____. What distinguishes this

remarkable individual from all others is _____

_____.

The most praiseworthy events in this person's life were _____

_____

_____.

Thus, if I had to draw a portrait of the ideal human I would

include the characteristics of _____

_____.

The activities this person would engage in would be _____

_____

_____.

Now, if I had to decide if this person would be happy, I would

say _____

_____ because _____

_____. Finally, if
I had to do one thing with my life tomorrow that would make me

more like this ideal human, it would be _____

_____.

Now, compare your image of the ideal human existence with
Aristotle's in the next two chapters. First underline important
parts of his summary in the next chapter and then number each
reason Aristotle presents to support his view that the happiest,
most fulfilled way of life is dedicated, in the broadest sense, to
philosophical contemplation. The subjects of this contemplation
would involve the sciences, mathematics, and the structure of
reality.

7. What is the relationship between happiness and philosophical contemplation?

1177a12

Now if happiness is the exercise of virtue, it is reasonable to suppose
that it will be the exercise of the highest virtue; and that will be the
virtue or excellence of the best part of us.

That part or faculty—call it reason or what you will—that seems
naturally to rule and take the lead in our personalities and to know
things noble and divine—whether it is divine, or only the divinest
part of us—is the faculty the exercise of which, in its proper excellence, will be perfect happiness.

That this consists in theoretical knowledge or philosophical
contemplation we have already said.

This conclusion seems to agree both with what we have said
above and with known truths.

This exercise of our faculty must be the highest possible because
reason is the highest of our faculties, and of all knowable things
those that reason deals with are the highest.

Again, it is the most continuous because contemplation can be
carried on more continuously than any other kind of action.

We think too that pleasure ought to be one of the ingredients of
happiness; but of all virtuous exercises it is agreed that the pleasantest is the exercise of theoretical wisdom. Philosophy is said to have
pleasures that are admirable in purity and steadfastness, and it is
reasonable to suppose that the time passes more pleasantly with
those who possess knowledge than with those who are seeking
knowledge.

Again, what is called self-sufficiency will be most of all found in
the activity concerned with theoretical wisdom. The necessities of
life, indeed, are needed by the wise man as well as by the just man.

But when these have been provided in an adequate quantity, the just man further needs persons toward whom, and along with whom, he may act justly; and so does the self-controlled man and the courageous man. The wise man, however, is able to contemplate truth even by himself, and the wiser he is the more he is able to do this. Perhaps he could do better if he had others to help him, but nevertheless he is more self-sufficient than anybody else.

Again, only the life of contemplation is desired solely for its own sake; it yields no result beyond the contemplation itself, while from all {other} actions we get something more or less besides the action itself.

Again, happiness is thought to imply leisure because we toil in order that we may have leisure, as we make war in order that we may enjoy peace. Now the practical virtues are exercised either in politics or in war, but these do not seem to be leisurely occupations.

War, indeed, seems to be quite the reverse of leisurely because no one chooses to fight for fighting's sake, or arranges a war for that purpose. He would be thought to be a bloodthirsty villain who would set friends at enmity in order that battles and slaughter might occur.

The politician's life also is not a leisurely occupation. The practice of politics seeks to bring power and honors, or at least happiness, to the politician and his fellow citizens. Thus, the practice of politics is not an end in itself.

The life of the politician and of the soldier, then, though they surpass all other virtuous exercises in nobility and grandeur, are not leisurely occupations, aim at some end beyond themselves, and are not desired merely for themselves.

Therefore the exercise of reason in pursuit of theoretical wisdom is superior in seriousness since it contemplates truth, aims at no end beside itself, and has its proper pleasure, which also helps increase the exercise of reason. Its exercise is self-sufficient, leisurely, and inexhaustible as far as anything human can be, and it has all the other characteristics that are ascribed to happiness.

This, then, will be the complete happiness of man, provided a complete span of life is added because nothing incomplete can be admitted into our idea of happiness.

But a life that realized this idea would be something more than human because it would not be the expression of man's nature, but of some divine element in that nature, exercise of which is as far superior to the exercise of the other kind of virtue {i.e., practical or moral virtue}, as this divine element is superior to our compound human nature.

If, then, reason is divine compared with man, the life that consists in the exercise of reason will also be divine in comparison with human life. Thus, instead of listening to those who advise us as men

Aristotle's main points thus far are:

_____

_____

_____

_____ .

1177b

What Aristotle is saying in this

paragraph is _____

_____

_____

_____

_____ .

and mortals not to lift our thoughts above what is human and mortal, we should instead as far as possible put off our mortality and make every effort to live in the exercise of the highest of our faculties, because though it be but a small part of us, yet in power and value it far surpasses all the rest.

And indeed this part even seems to constitute our true self, since it is the sovereign and the better part of us. It would be strange, then, if a man were to prefer the life of something else to the life of his true self.

Again, we may apply here what we said above: For every being what is best and pleasantest will be what is by nature proper to it. Since, then, it is the reason that in the truest sense is the man, the life that consists in the exercise of the reason in pursuit of theoretical wisdom is the best and pleasantest for man, and therefore the happiest.

Continue comparing your view of the ideal human life with Aristotle's in the next chapter.

8. What are the advantages of the contemplative life?

1178a8

Similarities between your ideal person and Aristotle's thus far are:

_____

_____

_____

_____

_____ .

Differences are: _____

_____

_____

_____

_____ .

The life that consists in the exercise of the other kind of virtue, moral virtue, is happy in a secondary sense because the manifestations of moral virtue are peculiarly human {not divine}. Justice, I mean, and courage, and the other moral virtues are displayed in our relations toward one another by the observance in every case of what is proper in contracts, services, and all sorts of outward acts, as well as in our inward feelings. And all these seem to be characteristically human affairs.

Again, moral virtue seems in some points actually to be a result of our bodily condition and in many points to be closely connected with the passions, and therefore it is inferior to the life of contemplation we just described.

Again, practical wisdom is inseparably joined to moral virtue, and moral virtue to practical wisdom, since the moral virtues determine the principles of practical wisdom, while practical wisdom determines what is right in morals.

Thus, because these virtues are bound up with the passions they must belong to our composite nature; and the virtues of our composite nature are peculiarly human. Therefore the life that manifests them, and the happiness that consists in this, must be peculiarly human and not like the near divine life of contemplation that we just described....

Further, the happiness produced by a life of contemplation needs only a small supply of external goods, certainly less than the moral life needs. Both need the necessaries of life to the same extent, let us say, because although the politician takes more care of his person than the philosopher, the difference will not be considerable. But in what they need for their activities there will be a great difference. Wealth will be needed by the generous man that he may act generously and by the just man to meet his obligations; the courageous man will need strength if he is to execute any deed of courage, but the wise man needs none of these kinds of things....

Underline reasons why "perfect happiness is some kind of contemplative activity."

Again, people dispute whether the moral purpose or the action be more essential to virtue, virtue being understood to imply both. It is plain, then, that both are necessary to completeness. Also, many things are needed for moral action, and the greater and nobler the action, the more is needed.

1178b

On the other hand, he who is engaged in contemplation needs none of these things for his work. It may even be said that they are a hindrance to contemplation, but as a man living with other men, he chooses to act virtuously. Thus he will need things of this sort to enable him to behave like other men.

That perfect happiness is some kind of contemplative activity may also be shown in the following way:

It is always supposed that the gods are, of all beings, the most blessed and happy; but what kind of actions shall we ascribe to them? Acts of justice? Surely it is ridiculous to conceive of the gods engaged in trade, returning deposits, and so on. Or acts of courage? Can we conceive them enduring fearful things and facing danger because it is noble to do so? Or acts of generosity? But to whom are they to give? Is it not absurd to suppose that they have money or anything of that kind? And what could acts of self-control mean with them? Surely it would be an insult to praise them for having no evil desires. In short, if we were to go through the whole list, we should find that all action is petty and unworthy of the gods.

And yet it is universally supposed that they live and, therefore, that they exert their powers, because we cannot suppose that they lie asleep like Endymion.

Now, if a being lives, and action cannot be ascribed to him, still less production, what remains but contemplation? It follows, then, that the divine life, which surpasses all others in blessedness, consists in contemplation.

Of all modes of human activity, therefore, whatever is most akin to the life of contemplation will be capable of the greatest happiness.

This is further confirmed by the fact that the other animals do not participate in happiness, being quite incapable of the life of contemplation. For the life of the gods is entirely blessed, and the life of man is blessed just so far as he attains to some likeness of the

Some reasons for Aristotle's conclusion that "happiness is a kind of contemplation" are: _____

_____

_____.

1179a

life of contemplation; but none of the other animals are happy, since they are quite incapable of contemplation.

Happiness, then, extends just so far as contemplation, and the more contemplation, the more happiness there is in a life.

Our conclusion, then, is that happiness is a kind of contemplation.

But as we are men we shall need external good fortune also, for our nature does not provide all that is necessary for contemplation. The body must be in health, and supplied with food, and otherwise cared for. We must not, however, suppose that because it is impossible to be happy without external good things, therefore a man who is to be happy will want many things. It is not an abundance of good things that makes a man self-sufficient, or enables him to act morally. A man may do noble deeds even though he is not a ruler of land and sea. A modest amount of possessions will give a man opportunity for virtuous action.

It is easy to find examples of this. Private citizens seem to do what is right not less but more than rulers....

Solon too, I think, gave a good description of the happy man when he said that, in his opinion, he was a man who was moderately supplied with the gifts of fortune but had done the noblest deeds and lived temperately, because a man who has only modest means is able to act virtuously.

Anaxagoras also seems to have held that the happy man was neither a rich man nor a ruler. He said that he would not be surprised if the happy man were one whom the masses could hardly believe to be so because they judge by the outside, which is all they can appreciate.

The opinions of the wise, then, seem to agree with our theory. But though these opinions carry some weight, the test of truth in matters of practice is to be found in the facts of life, because it is in them that the supreme authority resides. The theories we have advanced, therefore, should be tested by comparison with the facts of life. If they agree with the facts, they should be accepted, but if they disagree, they should be accounted mere theories.

But, once more, the man who exercises his reason, cultivates it, and has it in the best condition seems also to be the most beloved of the gods. For if the gods take any care for men, as they are thought to do, it is reasonable to suppose that they delight in what is best in man and most akin to themselves, that is, the reason, and that they reward those who show the greatest love and reverence for reason, as caring for what is dear to themselves and doing what is right and noble. But it is plain that all these points are found most of all in the wise man. The wise man, therefore, is the most beloved of the gods and therefore, we may conclude, the happiest.

1179a33

In this way also we have additional proof that the wise man will be happier than anyone else.

Now sum up Aristotle's argument about happiness and philosophical contemplation and then compare it with your own.

Stating Aristotle's position in the clearest and strongest way possible I would say _____

_____

_____.

For example, one of his most important points is "_____

_____."

Putting this in my own words I would say _____

_____.

The greatest strength of his view is _____

_____ because _____

_____.

The most significant weakness is _____

_____.

Trying to compare his view with mine, I see _____

_____

_____

_____.

As a way of summarizing these important chapters about the life of contemplation, compare a saint and someone who lives Aristotle's life of contemplation. For convenience, we will call this person a contemplative. Fill in the following chart with similarities and differences between the two.

	Saint	Contemplative
Source of happiness		
Major virtues		
Attitude toward possessions		
Attitude toward others		
Typical activities		
Personal characteristics		
Goal of life		

9. How can we become virtuous?

Underline the steps in Aristotle's answer to the title question.

1179b

Now that we have described these matters, and the virtues, and also friendship and pleasure, are we to suppose that we have attained the end we proposed? No, surely the saying is true that in practical matters the end is not mere speculative knowledge of what is to be done but the doing of it. It is not enough to know about virtue, then, but we must try to possess it, use it, and take any other steps that may make us good.

Now if theories had power in themselves to make us good, "many great rewards would they deserve," as Theognis says...; but in fact it seems that though theories are potent to guide and to stimulate generous-minded young men, and though a generous disposition, with a sincere love of what is noble, may be moved to virtuous action by theories of virtue, yet theories are powerless to turn the mass of men to goodness. For the mass of men are naturally apt to be swayed by fear rather than by reverence, and to refrain from wrongdoing because of the punishment that it brings rather than because of its own baseness. Under the rule of their passions the masses pursue the pleasures that suit their nature, and the means by which those pleasures may be obtained, and avoid the opposite pains. Of the noble and truly pleasant they have no idea because they have never tasted it.

What arguments, then, can change such men as these? Surely it is impossible, or at least very difficult, to remove by any argument what has long been ingrained in the character. For my part, I think we must be content if we can get some modest amount of virtue when all the circumstances are present that seem to make men good.

Now what makes men good is held by some to be nature, by others habit, by others teaching.

As for the goodness that comes by nature, it is plain that it is not within our control but is bestowed by some divine agency on certain people who truly deserve to be called fortunate. As for teaching, I fear that it is not successful in all cases, but the hearer's soul must be prepared by training to feel delight and aversion on the right occasions, just as the soil must be prepared if the seed is to thrive. If a man lives under the sway of his passions, he will not listen to arguments that try to change him, or even understand these arguments. When he is in this state of being ruled by his passions, how can you change his mind by argument? To put it bluntly, passion seems to yield to force only and not to reason. The individual's character, then, must be already formed, so that it has an affinity for virtue, loving what is noble and hating what is base.

But to get right guidance from our youth onward in the road to virtue is hard, unless we are brought up under the right laws. To live temperately and orderly is not pleasant to the mass of men, especially to the young. Our upbringing, then, and our whole way of life should be controlled by law, because it will cease to be painful as we get accustomed to it. I also think it is not enough to get proper training when we are young, but we ought to carry on the same way of life after we are grown up. We need the intervention of the law in these matters in our whole life. For the mass of men are more readily swayed by compulsion than by reason, and more by fear of punishment than by desire for what is noble.

1180a

Aristotle's view of the "mass of men" is _____ _____ _____.

For this reason some hold that the legislator should exhort and try to influence the people to be virtuous because of the nobility of virtue, because those who have been well trained will listen to him. But when the people will not listen, or are of less noble nature, the legislator should apply correction and punishment and banish those who are incorrigible. The good man, who takes what is noble as his guide, will listen to reason, but he who is not good, whose desires are set on pleasure, must be corrected by pain like a beast of burden. And for this reason also they say the pains to be applied must be those that are most contrary to the pleasures that the bad man loves.

As we have said, then, he who is to be good must be well brought up and trained and thereafter must continue in a virtuous way of life and must never either voluntarily or involuntarily do anything base. This can only be brought about if men live subject to some kind of reason and proper order, backed by force.

Now a father's rule does not have the necessary force or power, nor does the command of any individual, unless he is a king or something like one; but the law has a compulsory power and is a practical wisdom proceeding from a kind of rule of wisdom. And whereas we take offense at individuals who oppose our inclinations, even though their opposition is right, we do not feel aggrieved when the law bids us do what is right.

Sparta is, with a few exceptions, the only state where the legislator seems to have paid attention to the upbringing and mode of life of the citizens. In most states these matters are entirely neglected and each man lives as he likes, ruling wife and children like the Cyclops.[27]

It would be best, then, that the regulation of these matters should be undertaken and properly carried out by the state, but, as the state neglects it, it seems that we should each help (or at least, try to help) our own children or friends on the road to virtue.

Now it seems from what has been said that to enable one to do this, the best plan would be to learn how to legislate. For matters of common concern are carried on by means of laws and are good when the laws are good. It seems to make no difference whether the laws are written or unwritten, or whether they regulate the education of one person or many, any more than it does in the case of music, gymnastics, or any other course of training. For as in the state

1180b

what prevails is ordained by law and custom, so in the household what is ordained by the word of the father of the family and by custom prevails no less, or even more, because of the ties of kinship and of obligation. The reason for this is that affection and obedience are already implanted by nature in the members of the family.

Moreover, in spite of what has just been said, individual treatment is better than group treatment, in education no less than in medicine. As a general rule, rest and fasting are good for a fever patient, but in a particular case they may not be good. A teacher of boxing, I suppose, does not recommend everyone to adopt the same style. It seems, then, that individuals are educated more perfectly under a system of private education because then each gets more precisely what he needs.

But you will best be able to treat an individual case, whether you are a doctor, a trainer, or anything else, when you know the general rule, "Such and such a thing is good for all men," or "for all of a certain temperament"; for science is said to deal, and does deal, with what is common to a number of individuals.

I do not mean to deny that it may be quite possible to treat an individual well even without any scientific knowledge, if you know precisely by experience the effect of particular causes on him, just as some men seem to be able to treat themselves better than any doctor, though they would be quite unable to prescribe to another person.

Nevertheless I believe that if a man wishes to master any art or gain a scientific knowledge of it, he must proceed to its general principles and make himself acquainted with them in the proper method. As we have said, it is with universal propositions that the sciences deal.

Aristotle's conclusion in this

paragraph is _____

_____

_____

_____ .

And so I think that he who wishes to make men better by training, whether many or few, should try to acquire the art or science of legislation, supposing that men may be made good by the agency of law. To mold the character of any person who may present himself is not a thing that can be done by anybody, but, if at all, only by him who has knowledge, just as is the case in medicine and other professions where careful treatment and practical wisdom are required.

The next topic is _____

_____

_____

_____ .

Our next business, then, is to inquire from whom or by what means we are to learn the science or art of legislation. It is in the same way as we learn the other arts, from the experts in those arts, in this case from the politicians who practice it, for we found that legislation is part of politics.

But I think the case is not quite the same with politics as with the other sciences and arts. In other cases it is plain that the same people communicate the art and practice it, as physicians and painters do; in the case of politics, while the Sophists profess to teach the art, it is never they that practice it but the statesmen. And the statesmen seem to act by some instinctive faculty, proceeding empirically rather than by reasoning. For it is plain that they never write or speak about these matters, though perhaps that would be better than making speeches in the courts or the assembly, and have never communicated that art to their sons or any of their friends. And yet we might expect that they would have done so if they could, because they could have left no better legacy to their country or have chosen anything more precious than this power as a possession for themselves and, therefore, for those dearest to them.

Experience, however, seems to be of great service here, because otherwise people would never become statesmen by familiarity with politics. Those who wish for a knowledge of statesmanship, then, seem to need experience as well as theory.

But those Sophists who profess to teach statesmanship seem to be ludicrously incapable of fulfilling their promises. To speak plainly, they do not even know what it is or what it deals with. If they did know, they would not make it identical with rhetoric, or inferior to it, nor would they think it was easy to frame a system of laws when you had made a collection of the most approved existing laws. "It is but a matter of picking out the best," they say, ignoring the fact that this selection requires understanding and that to judge correctly is a matter of the greatest difficulty here, as in music. Those who have special experience in any department can pass a correct judgment on the result and understand how and by what means it is produced and what combinations are harmonious. Those who have no special experience must be content if they are able to say whether the result is good or bad, as, for instance, in the case of painting. Now laws are the work or result of statesmanship. How then could a collection of laws make a man able to legislate or to pick out the best of the collection?

Even the art of healing, it seems, cannot be taught by collections of rules. And yet the medical collections of rules try to tell you not only the remedies but also how to apply them and how to treat the different classes of patients, distinguishing them according to their temperament. But all this, though it may be serviceable to those who have experience, seems to be quite useless to those who know nothing about medicine.

So also, I think we may say, collections of laws and constitutions may be very serviceable to those who are able to examine them with a discriminating eye and to judge whether an ordinance is good or bad and what ordinances agree with one another; but if people who do not have the trained ability go through such collections of rules, they cannot judge properly unless indeed a correct judgment comes of itself, though they may perhaps sharpen their intelligence in these matters.

Since our predecessors have left this matter of legislation unin-
vestigated, it will perhaps be better to inquire into it ourselves, and
indeed into the whole question of the management of a state, in
order that our philosophy of human life may be completed to the
best of our power.

Let us try, then, first of all to consider any utterances that our
predecessors have made about this or that branch of the subject and
then to look at our collection of constitution, and {try to discern}
what the causes are of good government of some states and the
misgovernment of others, for when we have an insight into these
matters, we shall, I think, be better able to see what is the best kind
of constitution and what is the best arrangement of each of the
different kinds—that is to say, what system of laws and customs is
best suited to each.

Let us begin then.[28]

One of the most interesting points Aristotle makes in Book X is
that that it is not enough to understand what a virtuous life is;
one needs to become virtuous. He also points out early in the
Nicomachean Ethics that one becomes virtuous by doing virtuous
actions. You have now read one of the classic ethical documents
in the history of philosophy, analyzed it rather closely, and
constructed your own vision of the ideal human. Now it is time
for you to make a plan about how to live more virtuously. To
simplify this I have constructed a table that divides your life into
several areas. Briefly describe, for each area, what virtuous action
would be in general and then one new and specific thing you
could do to become more virtuous. Borrow ideas from Aristotle
wherever appropriate.

AN ANALYSIS OF MY LIFE

	In general virtuous action involves...	A new, specific action would be
School		
Work		
Relations with friends		
Home		
Leisure		

The next step would be to try out some of the actions you suggested to yourself and perhaps keep a daily diary about the results. I think Aristotle is right when he argues that happiness involves virtuous action, and virtuous action does make one happy. Thus one index of your success ought to be whether it produces happiness. I have given students this diary assignment several times in the last few years, and for many it has produced surprisingly positive results. This would not surprise Aristotle; in essence you will be letting reason, the most divine element in your nature, guide your life.

Appendix A
Writing a Short Essay about Aristotle

Here is a chapter from Book IX of the *Nicomachean Ethics*. We will go slowly through this, stop after each key section, and think together about the important points. In effect you will be putting together notes to use in constructing a short essay.

8. Should we love ourselves more than we love others?

Another question that is raised is, should we love ourselves more than others?

We blame, it is said, those who love themselves most, and apply the term *self-loving* to them as a term of reproach. Also, he who is not good is thought to think of himself in everything that he does, and the worse he is, the more he thinks of himself. Thus we accuse him of doing nothing without self-interest. On the other hand, it is thought that the good man takes what is noble as his motive, and the better he is the more he is guided by this motive and, out of regard for his friend, neglects his own interest.

What is the distinction Aristotle says people make between a good man and a base man in relation to self-love?

A base man is one who _____

_____. A good man appears to

be one who _____.

The main point he is making about what some people believe

about self-love is _____

_____.

    In the next section, note and underline the points Aristotle makes against the view in the first section. In the first section he states one kind of popular view, and in the following he begins to develop another.

    But this theory disagrees with facts, nor is it surprising that it does, for it is agreed that we should love him most who is most truly a friend. He is most truly a friend who, in wishing well to another, wishes well to him for his, the other's, sake, even though no one should ever know this. But all these characteristics, and all the others that go to make up the definition of a friend, are found in the highest degree in a man's relations to himself. We have already seen how it is from our relations to ourselves that all our friendly relations to others are derived. Moreover, all the proverbs point to the same conclusion—such as "Friends have one soul," "Friends have all things in common," "Equality makes friendship," "Charity begins at home." All these characteristics are found in the highest degree in a man's relations to himself, because he is his own best friend. Thus he must love himself better than anyone else.

    People are not unnaturally puzzled to know which of these two positions {loving ourselves more or loving others more} to adopt, since both appeal to them.

Now, Aristotle has presented two views about self-love. What points does he make in the second section?

    His main points in the second section are: _____

_____.

In the first section he is saying self-love is _____

because _____.

By contrast, in the second section he says self-love is _____

because _____.

    Aristotle has a small philosophical problem. Whenever possible, he prefers to make his views harmonize with the views of others. The problem is that at this point, some say self-love is good and some say self-love is bad. Aristotle finds a way of agreeing with both! Read the next section and see how he begins to develop his analysis.

Perhaps the best method of dealing with conflicting statements of this kind is to analyze them and clearly distinguish how far and in what sense each is right. So here, if we first determine what *self-loving* means in each statement, the difficulty will perhaps be cleared up.

Those who use *self-loving* as a criticism apply the name to those who take more than their share of money, honor, and bodily pleasures, because the mass of men desire these things and set their hearts on them as the best things in the world, so they are keenly competed for. Those, then, who grasp at more than their share of these things indulge their animal appetites and their passions generally—in a word, the irrational part of their nature. This is the character of the mass of men and hence the term *self-loving* has come to be used in this bad sense from the fact that the greater part of mankind are not good. It is with justice, then, that we find fault with those who are self-loving in this sense.

It can be easily shown that it really is to those who take more than their share of these things that the term is usually applied by the mass of men.

What kind of self-love has he just described?

A key sentence is "_____

_____."

The kind of self-love he is describing is _____

_____.

Underline a different kind of self-love he describes in the next section. Number each of the major points he makes.

If what a man always set his heart on were that he rather than another should do what is just, temperate, or in any other way virtuous—if, in a word, he were always claiming the noble course of conduct, no one would call him self-loving, and no one would find fault with him.

And yet such a man seems to be more truly self-loving. At least he takes for himself what is noblest and most truly good and satisfies the ruling power {of reason} in himself and in all things obeys it. But just as the ruling part in a state or in any other system seems more than any other part to be the state or the system {itself}, so also the ruling part of a man seems to be most truly the man's self. Therefore he who loves and satisfies this part of himself is most truly self-loving.

Again, we call a man morally strong or morally weak based on whether his reason has the ruling part, implying that his reason is the same as himself. When a man has acted under the guidance of his reason, he is thought, in the fullest sense, to have done the deed himself and of his own will.

It is plain, then, that this part of us is our self, or is most truly our self, and that the good man more than any other loves this part of himself. He, then, more than any other, will be self-loving, in another sense than the man whom we fault as self-loving, differing from him by all the difference that exists between living according to reason and living according to passion, between desiring what is noble and desiring what appears to be profitable.

Those who more than other men set their hearts on noble deeds are welcomed and praised by all. But if all men were competing with each other in the pursuit of what is noble and were straining every nerve to act in the noblest possible manner, the result would be that the needs of the community would be perfectly satisfied, and at the same time each individual would achieve virtue, which is the greatest of all good things.

He is saying?
    As opposed to the previous kind of self-love, this second kind

is _____.

He makes this point clearly when he says, "_____
_____." In effect he is

saying _____
_____.

A good example would be _____
_____.

    You are becoming a good example of a carefully slow thinker. In the concluding section underline important points and put your own paraphrases in the column.

The good man, therefore, ought to be self-loving, because by doing what is noble he will at once benefit himself and others. The bad man should not {be self-loving}, because he will injure both himself and his neighbors by following passions that are not good.

Thus with the bad man there is a discrepancy between what he should do and what he does, but with the good man what he should do is what he does because reason always chooses what is best for itself, and the good man obeys the voice of reason.

Again, it is quite true to say of the good man that he does many things for the sake of his friends and his country and will even die for them if need be. He will throw away money, honor, and, in a word, all the good things for which men compete, claiming the noble for himself. He will prefer a brief period of intense pleasure to a long period of mild pleasure, one year of noble life to many years of ordinary life, one great and noble action to many little ones. This, we may perhaps say, is what he gets who gives his life for others. Thus, he chooses for himself something that is noble on a grand scale.

Such a man will surrender wealth to enrich his friend, for while his friend gets money, he gets what is noble. In this way he takes the greater good for himself.

His conduct will be the same with regard to honors and offices. He will give up all to his friend because he believes this is noble and praiseworthy.

Such a man, then, is not unreasonably considered good, as he chooses what is noble in preference to everything else.

But, again, it is possible to give up to your friend an opportunity for action, and it may be nobler to cause your friend to do a deed than to do it yourself.

It is plain, then, that in all cases in which he is praised the good man takes for himself a larger share of what is noble. And in this sense, as we have said, a man ought to be self-loving, but not in the sense in which the mass of men are self-loving.

Make your own notes about this final section.

The major points were _____

_____.

Here is the hard question. Aristotle began by describing two contradictory views of self-love. In the first case, he presented the view that one shouldn't be self-loving. Then he presented arguments that held the opposite. How did he end up agreeing with both views?

Simply put, one ought to be self-loving if one means by self-love _____

_____ and one ought not to be self-loving if one means by self-love _____

_____.

Now we are ready to begin designing your short essay. First you need a thesis. Obviously it will have something to do with Aristotle's analysis of the two kinds of self-love.

I could start with, "According to Aristotle _____

_____."

Or, "In Book IX of the *Nicomachean Ethics* Aristotle _____

_____."

Or, "The Aristotelian view of self-love involves _____

_____."

Or, "_____

_____."

    The body of your essay probably has at least five major parts. Just as you began to do above, first you would discuss Aristotle's description of the popular view of self-love as bad, and a second popular view of self-love as good. The third part of the body would begin with a transition describing how Aristotle is going to try to solve the problem of agreeing with both views. This part of the body would continue to present the sense in which self-love can be said to be bad. The fourth part of the body would develop Aristotle's view of the noble forms of self-love. By "develop" I mean quote sections from Aristotle, put them in your own words, add your own examples, explain how the examples relate to the general point you are making. You have been practicing many of these steps all through this tour. The final section of the body would involve your evaluation of the strengths and weaknesses of Aristotle's argument. Your introduction should begin with your thesis and then briefly describe each of these parts of the body.

    My thesis would be something like "_____

_____

_____."

The next sentences should give a brief overview of the body of the paper, which will illustrate this thesis. I could say something

like "_____

_____

_____

_____."

Of course, I could make that clearer with several revisions.

    Good start. Now make a list of the points you want to make in each of the five parts of the body.

    In part one of the body I will mention _____

_____.

In part two I will talk about the following: _____

_____.

Part three will begin with a transition something like: "_____

_____,"

and then I will go on to make the following points describing

Aristotle's argument _____

_____.

In part four I will try to describe each of Aristotle's main argu-

ments, just as I did in the other parts. I will talk about _____

_____

_____. Then, in part five I will talk

about the strengths of his argument. Right now I would say

_____

_____.

The weaknesses I want to think about are _____

_____.

Now you are finished with your outline. Before you actually
write this short essay you should go back and read Chapter 9
several more times, underline essential sections, write your own
remarks in the column, think up good examples, and begin to
expand your notes into sentences and paragraphs.

One last piece of advice. As I look over Aristotle's description
of self-love I think the most difficult part of your essay will be
section four. Aristotle presents quite a few arguments in favor of
the noble form of self-love and illustrates this praiseworthy
emotion with numerous examples. When you start section four
you might begin with a mini-introduction like, "Aristotle presents (whatever number you decide) arguments in favor of a
noble form of self-love." Then go on to list and elaborate each.

Appendix B
An Aristotelian Journal

The *Nicomachean Ethics* contain a wealth of topics one could fruitfully think about. The advantage of keeping a journal as a way of thinking is that writing is seldom a circular process. I've often noted that I can think the same thought over and over, but when I write it down it grows into something else, often something surprising. Here are five beginnings you might use to start journal entries.

1. Aristotle says most actions are means to some end. What ends are my actions headed toward?

I would have to say _____

_____.

2. The *Nicomachean Ethics* ends with a description of philosophical contemplation as the highest and most satisfactory human activity. What would be my last chapter if I created an ethical system?

I would start by describing _____

_____.

3. {This would continue an earlier exercise.} The problem, says Aristotle, is not just to understand virtue but to start *being* virtuous. Very well, first I need to define what I mean by a truly virtuous life and then create a step-by-step plan, a series of means, to attain that end.

I would say virtue involves _____

_____.

4. If I were to pattern my life on anyone it would be _____
_____ because _____
_____.

The first things I would do differently would be _____
_____.

5. Let me look into my own heart. What virtues and what vices of excess or deficiency do I see there?

I will start with _____
_____.

6. The most troubling thing about the *Nicomachean Ethics* was
_____.

Or, you might like to try to answer any of the following questions.

What did I learn from Aristotle that is worth remembering?

What did I read about that I need to think about more carefully?

What do I desire as a means to some other means? What do I desire as truly an end in itself?

Do I have a tendency to commit more vices of deficiency or excess? Why and/or when?

What virtues did I honestly recognize in myself as I read the *Nicomachean Ethics?* How can I strengthen these?

What virtues are missing from Aristotle's ethics?

Am I entirely responsible for all my actions?

Can I turn any means into ends? Should I? Should I change any ends?

What are my intellectual virtues and vices?

What did Aristotle say that seemed obviously true? Obviously false? What do I need to think more about?

Aristotle's World

399 B.C.	Socrates dies (born 470 B.C.). Plato is Socrates' student from 407 to 399.
395	Thucydides, Greek historian, author of *The Peloponnesian Wars*, dies.
387	Plato writes *Symposium*.
	Aristophanes, Greek playwright of the "old comedy," dies. In his *The Clouds* Socrates is lampooned.
384	**Aristotle is born.**
	Demosthenes, Greek statesman and orator, is born.
380–343	The Thirtieth Dynasty of Egypt is the last native house to rule the country.
377	Hippocrates of Cos, Greek physician, formulator of the Hippocratic Oath, dies (born 460 B.C.).
	Around this time iron comes into use as a working material in China.
	Walls are built around the city of Rome for defense.
371	Xenophon writes *Anabasis*, the account of his adventures with the Greek mercenary armies fighting for Cyrus in Persia.
366	First plebian is elected to office of consul in Rome.
365	Etruscan actors stage first theater in Rome.
356	Alexander the Great, son of Philip II of Macedonia, is born.
352	Philip II of Macedonia comes to the throne.

Mahabharata, Indian heroic epic, is being written. Writing will continue until 350 A.D.

c. 350	Corinthian columns appear in Greek architecture.
347	Plato dies.
343	**Aristotle becomes tutor of Alexander.**
	Persians reconquer Egypt.
340	Epicurus, founder of the Epicurean school of philosophy, is born.
	Praxagorus of Cos discovers the difference between arteries and veins.
338	Philip II of Macedonia defeats Greek allies at Chaeronea.
	First Roman coins appear.
336	Assassination of Philip of Macedonia; he is succeeded by Alexander the Great.
	Assassination of Arses of Persia; accession of Darius III. Alexander will fight Darius for the Persian Empire.
	Zeno of Citium founds the Stoic school of philosophy.
335	**Aristotle returns to Athens and founds "peripatetic" school of philosophy,** i.e., doing philosophy while walking around in the open.
	Alexander destroys Thebes.
333	Alexander the Great campaigns against Darius III and Persia, defeats Darius at Issus.
332	Alexander conquers Tyre and Jerusalem, founds port of Alexandria.
331	Alexander defeats Darius at Gaugamela.
330	Alexander occupies Babylon, Susa, and Persepolis.
	Darius III murdered by his own court. Alexander gives him a royal burial.
	Pytheas of Marsilia (Marseilles) reaches Britain.
	Praxiteles, Greek sculptor, dies (born 400 B.C.).
328	Alexander marries Boetian princess Roxana.
326	Alexander invades India.
324	Alexander extends his empire to Indus River, then his generals force him to turn back.
323	Alexander dies in Babylon; his empire is partitioned among his generals.
	Euclid produces *Elements,* the standard work on geometry.

New Egyptian Dynasty begins under the Greek Ptolemy, one of Alexander's generals. The dynasty will last until the death of Cleopatra in 30 B.C.

322	**Aristotle dies.**
	Demosthenes commits suicide.
321	War breaks out between Alexander's successors.
320–330	The Hellenistic period of Greek art.

Aristotle's Life

384 B.C. Aristotle is born at Stagira. He is born into a moderately well-to-do family. Aristotle's father is a physician who served at the Macedonian court at Pella. He dies early, and the young Aristotle is brought up by relatives in Atarneus in Asia Minor.

367–366 At seventeen Aristotle goes to Athens to study at Plato's academy. Plato is in Sicily and Eudoxus of Cnidus is the acting head of the school. Some of Eudoxus' thoughts are evident in the *Nicomachean Ethics*.

348–347 Plato dies. Aristotle leaves Athens with Xenocrates, a school colleague. They are invited by Hermias of Atarneus to settle there. Hermias offers Aristotle and Xenocrates land to start a new school in Assos. For an unknown reason, Aristotle leaves and starts a school at Mytelene on the island of Lesbos.

343–342 After two years at Mytelene Aristotle is invited to Pella by Philip II of Macedonia (Aristotle's father's connections are evidently influential) to become tutor to his son Alexander, who will soon be called "the Great." Three years later the tutorship ends as Aristotle is drawn into Macedonian affairs. He then moves back to Stagira, his birthplace. Stagira had been destroyed eight years before Aristotle's return but Philip and Alexander had the town rebuilt in Aristotle's honor.

335–334 Aristotle moves to Athens once more and for twelve years teaches and writes at the lyceum. His career there ends with the death of Alexander in Babylon in June of

323 B.C. When the news of Alexander's death reaches Athens there is an open revolt to Macedonian rule, and Aristotle falls from favor because of his loyalties to Alexander. A charge of impiety is brought against him for composing a hymn in memory of Alexander. Aristotle leaves Athens before a trial can develop. As one tradition has it, Aristotle left so that Athens would be "spared commiting a sin against philosophy a second time." (In 399 B.C. the Athenians had condemned Socrates to death for impiety.) Aristotle flees with his family to Chalcis, his mother's birthplace.

322   In November Aristotle dies at the age of sixty-two at Chalcis soon after leaving Athens.

Notes

1. W. T. Jones, *History of Western Philosophy: The Classical Mind*.

2. However, both teleological and deontological ethical systems should be distinguished from what has come to be called an "ethics of virtue." This approach emphasizes the connection of traditional virtues like courage and friendship to social roles within a community. Honor is considered a key concept, because it is through the bestowing of honor that a society retains its cohesiveness. This approach considers ethics to be much more than mastering a set of ethical rules; it involves habitually acting on those rules.

3. The Greek word that Aristotle uses is *eudaimonie,* which is generally translated as *happiness.* The word derives from the Greek *eu* (the adverb of *good*), meaning "well," and *daimon,* meaning approximately "genius" or "destiny." Modern translations at variance with *happiness* generally use *well-being* or *human flourishing.*

4. The Greek word that Aristotle uses here is *techne.* The Greek noun *techne* is generally translated as either *art* or *craft.* Less frequent translations include *skill* and *trade.* We retain the general sense of the term in the English word *technology.*

5. Plato argued that there is an unchanging realm that is constituted only by what he called Forms. The Form of the Good is the one Form that is responsible for the reality and the knowability of the other Forms. All things that we know with our senses, according to Plato, are inferior copies of Forms.

6. Sardanapalus is the Greek name for Ashurhanipal, king of Assyria in the seventh century B.C. He is often taken, as Aristotle presents him here, as a classic example of the pleasure seeker.

7. The discussion Aristotle refers to is found in the *Ethics* at 1177a12–1178a8 and 1178a22–1179a32.

8. Aristotle found it difficult to criticize the Theory of Forms, for which Plato, his teacher, was most famous.

9. Aristotle's understanding of the good should be contrasted with Plato's Form of the Good. Aristotle believed our own actions can lead us to the good; Plato believed the Good could never be attained by human actions.

10. The "Delian inscription" refers to the saying of the oracle on the temple of Apollo on the island of Delos in the Aegean Sea.

11. The Greek *ethos* means "habit." Other translations include *custom, usage,* or *manners.* This fits with Aristotle's view that moral virtue, or virtue of character, is only genuine when it is a habit of acting in accordance with right desire.

12. This discussion takes place in Book VI, Chapter 13.

13. The Greek is *anaisthetos,* which literally means "without perception." *Extremely inhibited, unfeeling,* or *insensible* seem appropriate translations.

14. Thinking in terms of the genus and species is characteristic of Aristotle. The former refers to what is common of all members of a class, in this case the virtues, and what they hold in common is that they are all states. The later refers to what differentiates the members, in this case, what differentiates the virtues.

15. The Greek is *megalopsychia,* which literally means "greatness of soul." *Magnanimous* would be an alternate translation.

16. The Greek is *micropsychia,* which literally means "smallness of soul." *Meanness of spirit* would be an alternate translation.

17. Calypso was a nymph in Homer's *Odyssey* who detained Odysseus in Ogygia for seven years. (*Od.* 22.219) Actually, Circe gave the advice and the quotation is from Odysseus' orders to his steersman.

18. The reference is to the *Iliad* of Homer. (*Il.* 3.156–60) Helen was the beautiful daughter of Zeus and Leda and the wife of Menelaus. Her abduction by Paris was the cause of the Trojan War.

19. Euripides' play is lost. According to Greek mythology, Alcmaeon killed his mother to avenge the death of his father. These were the circumstances that "forced" his action.

20. Aristotle's point is that desire can overpower choice because they struggle with one another in the soul, whereas desires do not struggle with one another in the soul.

21. Virtuous actions are the mean between excess and defect. For example, with respect to the feeling of fear, the excess is cowardice, the defect is foolhardiness, and the mean is courage.

22. The reference is to a Greek lyric and elegiac poet of Iulis on the Aegean island of Ceos who lived circa 500 B.C. In a short lyric entitled "The Precariousness of Prosperity," Simonides warns that humans cannot predict the future, and prosperity is fleeting. This explains why Aristotle claims that Simonides would not approve of the "generous" man who does not value wealth.

23. The Greek is *kuminopristes,* which literally means "one who saws cumin seed in half."

24. Heraclitus was a pre-Socratic Greek philosopher whose fundamental view was that everything in the world is changing all the time. His famous line, "You can't step into the same river twice," is intended to illustrate this doctrine, called the doctrine of flux. Aristotle thought this view to be absurd and often uses Heraclitus as an example of one who holds improbable theories.

25. In the *Protagoras* Socrates argued that it is not possible for a man to act against knowledge. To know what justice is is to act justly. Aristotle is here acknowledging that Socrates was in some sense correct.

26. Eudoxus of Cnidus joined forces with Plato's academy for some time around 367 B.C. Eudoxus was influential both as an astronomer and as a philosopher who championed hedonism, the view that pleasure is the good.

27. The reference is to Homer's *Odyssey,* in which the Cyclops were represented as savage one-eyed giants living without laws or government.

28. Many critics believe this last section, which unites ethical considerations to political ones, was added by a later editor of the *Nicomachean Ethics.*

Bibliography

Greene, M. *A Portrait of Aristotle.* Chicago: University of Chicago Press, 1963. Greene's book is a good one-volume introduction to Aristotle. She makes a persuasive argument that Aristotle's passion for biology is a key to understanding his work.

Jones, W. T. *The Classical Mind: A History of Western Philosophy.* New York: Harcourt Brace Jovanovich, 1969. This is probably the best beginning place for an introduction to Aristotle. Jones, as always, presents a clear overview and incorporates useful information about the Greek cultural background.

Ross, W. D. *Aristotle*, 5th ed. New York: Harper & Row, 1964. A classic account of Aristotle's work by one of his best known modern translators.

Urmson, J. O. *Aristotle's Ethics.* New York: Oxford University Press, 1988. A good, short (130 pages) introduction to Aristotle's ethics.